Additional Praise for *Becoming Your Own China Stock Guru*

"This book is a must read for anyone interested in China and even considering it! Jim Trippon's track record of picking winning stocks is remarkable. I have known Jim personally and he truly is a guru. Anyone remotely interested in China should own this book."

—Marc Siegel, President, China Direct, AMEX (CDS)

"China's financial system has gone from the brink of collapse a few short years ago to an economic powerhouse with arms that stretch around the world. In *Becoming Your Own China Stock Guru,* Jim Trippon shows how serious investors can reap the rewards of China's fast-growing economy."

—Don Stowers, Editor, *Oil & Gas Financial Journal*

"Jim's grasp of the historic, cultural, and economic forces shaping the current Chinese market, and its challenges, helps lift the veil of wonderment and points to opportunities for all investors."

—Tom Hudson, First Business TV

Becoming Your Own China Stock Guru

THE ULTIMATE INVESTOR'S GUIDE TO PROFITING FROM CHINA'S ECONOMIC BOOM

James Trippon

WILEY

John Wiley & Sons, Inc.

Published by John Wiley & Sons, Inc., Hoboken, New Jersey.
Published simultaneously in Canada.

For general information on our other products and services or for technical support, please contact our Customer Care Department within the United States at (800) 762-2974, outside the United States at (317) 572-3993, or fax (317) 572-4002.

Wiley also publishes its books in a variety of electronic formats. Some content that appears in print may not be available in electronic books. For more information about Wiley products, visit our web site at www.wiley.com.

Library of Congress Cataloging-in-Publication Data

Trippon, James.
    Becoming your own China stock guru: the ultimate investor's guide to profiting from China's economic boom/James Trippon.
        p. cm.
    Includes index.
    ISBN 978-0-470-22312-3 (cloth)
        1. Investments—China. 2. Stocks—China. 3. Investments, Foreign—China. 4. China—Economic conditions—1976-2000. 5. China—Economic conditions—2000- I. Title.
    HG5782. T725 2008
    332.63'220951—dc22

                                                                2007044840

Printed in the United States of America.
10 9 8 7 6 5 4 3 2 1

For my Children . . .
May you be wise enough
to make a changing future your servant,
and never your master.

Contents

Acknowledgments

Writing a book, like any great effort, requires a team. There are countless people who helped me along my path and allowed the idea for this book to become a reality. First and foremost, thanks to my dear wife, Kim, who tolerates my extended absences while I scour China for new investment opportunities.

Very special thanks go to my *China Stock Digest* team, especially Johnson Zhang and Professor Wu in Shanghai, Eric in Hong Kong, Susanne in Shenzhen, Gyan in Beijing, and George Wolff, Gigi Guthrie, Amal Zaid, and Ramona Moreno in the United States. Thanks also to Bernie Joseph, who runs my team in the Philippines.

To Sam Juneau, one of the few Renaissance men of our age, I owe tremendous respect and admiration. I also wish to acknowledge James Wolfenson, past president of the World Bank, whose insights about the future of China have greatly broadened my understanding about the most dynamic economy on the planet.

I also owe a great deal to my friend Dan Nip, who has assisted me immeasurably in his capacity as the president of the Houston-Shenzhen Sister City Association. Thanks as well to Jim and Kathi Austin and my fellow board members at the Houston International Festival. I must also acknowledge the contributions of my friends at Houston's Asian Chamber of Commerce, especially Elsie Huang, and thank my fellow members of the Petroleum Club of Houston. I also greatly appreciate the help I have received from Dong Chunming at the Chinese Magnesium Association, Connie Pang at the Shekou Container Terminals, Ltd., Ben Toh at the Venetian Macau, Ermanno Pascutto at Troutman Sanders Hong Kong, and Liu Fuzhong at the Shenzhen Stock Exchange.

I find great peace with the help of my friends at Chapelwood UMC, especially Jim Jackson, Wick Stuckey, and Dale Dodds. The same is true of Joel Osteen at Lakewood Church and my Iron Men brothers at the Second Baptist Church.

To my publishing world friends: I wish to say thank you to the whole team at John Wiley & Sons, as well as to John Willig at Literary Services, Inc., Don Nicholas at Mequoda, Ed Finn at *Barron's*, Bob Bly, Peter Fogel, James DiGiorgia, Paul Krupin, and the Harrison Brothers at Radio-TV Interview Report, and last, but never least, Steven Halpern at AOL Finance.

Special thanks go to my media friends, including Tom Hudson at First Business, the entire gang at CNBC, Fox News, the Fox Business Network, and CNN International. I also gained valuable insight from Don Stowers at the *Oil & Gas Financial Journal*, Kira Brecht at *SFO Magazine*, Deborah Duncan and Peggy Tuck in Houston, and Andy Giersher at WBBM Chicago. Thanks for your recognition and advice to Mark Hulbert at the *Hulbert Financial Digest*. And a salute also goes to Donald Trump, who has made being rich fashionable again.

I also owe a debt of gratitude to those writers and journalists who make me and our fellow countrymen think: Bill O'Reilly, Lou Dobbs, Wolf Blitzer, William J. O'Neal, Paul Kangas, Ann Coulter, Anderson Cooper, Ted Koppel, Laura Ingraham, Jean Chatzky, and Tim Russert. I would be remiss if I failed to acknowledge Charles Githler and Howard Gold, who have opened new horizons in the financial universe to the public at the World Money Show. Thanks also go to Steve Crowley, the voice and the brains of the American Scene radio broadcast and to Jon Stewart and Stephen Colbert, who not only make us think, but also allow us to laugh while doing so.

Finally, I wish to thank anyone who has helped me appreciate, understand, and write about the Chinese economic phenomenon but may have been omitted because of a lack of space or an inadvertent lapse of memory.

I hope in these acknowledgments to live up to the wisdom of Confucius, who wrote, "Forget injuries, never forget kindnesses." I must say I have enjoyed a great many kindnesses on my remarkable voyage of discovery in China. I thank the Chinese people, who have endured so much and yet succeeded so magnificently.

About the Author

Jim Trippon is America's foremost authority on successful China investing. Trippon serves as editor-in-chief for the *China Stock Digest*, America's top-performing Chinese investment newsletter. A former Pricewaterhouse CPA, Jim has worked extensively inside China and has invested in its financial markets for years. Trippon manages a full-time team of financial analysts in China from his offices in Houston and throughout China.

Trippon runs the Trippon Wealth Management Group, LLC, an SEC Registered Investment Advisory that works with corporate pension plans, private trusts, and some of America's wealthiest families to implement China investment strategies.

Trippon, his wife, and children reside in Houston, Texas.

For a complimentary issue of Trippon's *China Stock Digest* newsletter, visit chinastockdigest.com.

Introduction

When I was young, I used to think that money was the most important thing in life. Now that I am old, I know it is.
—Oscar Wilde

If you're reading this introduction while still in the bookstore and are considering buying this book, let me ask you a question: Does the idea of the United States losing its status as the world's largest manufacturing superpower bother you? What will this mean to your family's financial future? We are at a watershed moment in world history. The greatest economic superpower the world has ever seen is being born right now. China's economic revolution is only three decades old and it is already changing the investment landscape of the world. The moment you opened this book, you opened the door to the most significant financial opportunity since the emergence of the United States as an industrial power.

My goal is to help you make money from the Chinese economic miracle. I know for a fact that China offers you more profit potential than you could ever enjoy by limiting your investment choices to the U.S. stock market. How can I be so sure?

I know from experience. So do the subscribers to my monthly newsletter, the *China Stock Digest* (for a free sample issue, visit my web site at chinastockdigest.com). Many subscribers say that following my China investment research was the best financial decision they ever made. They, too, have experienced the amazing returns that investing in a supercharged economy can bring.

I'm also here to reassure you that investing in the mysterious East doesn't have to be mysterious at all. My job is to make the process simple. With this book, I intend to take the mystery out of the process. I wish to pave the way for you to profit from a huge economic event . . . an event that has already taken the steam out of some familiar American companies.

How can I say confidently that the new Chinese economy is an appropriate target for our investment dollars? Some readers may worry about China's chaotic and tragic past. Today, China is still a one-party state, run by Communist Party officials. So how can capitalism thrive and earn double-digit returns for investors under a communist banner? As I will show you, the proof is in the pudding. China is delivering spectacular returns, and continues to grow at an enviable rate.

Now, my guess is that most readers will not be able to name a single investment-grade Chinese company. After all, there are hundreds of Chinese firms listed on American stock markets; some are very profitable and some are very speculative investments. I will help you learn how to tell them apart.

Most U.S. investors have developed a level of comfort investing in U.S. firms. As such, it's no surprise that the very idea of placing our hard-earned dollars in the hands of companies on the other side of the world can be a bit daunting. But remember, the golden rule of investing is diversification. There's nothing magic about U.S. companies or the U.S. economy. In fact, there is a real risk in putting all your eggs into any single basket, in the United States or in China.

Scan any newspaper on any given day and you'll see plenty of disturbing reports about deep structural problems in the U.S. economy. The dollar is weakening against most world currencies. Our nation's deficits are deep and the U.S. government is not taking action to remedy problems that the Comptroller General of the United States calls "potentially disastrous." That's why diversification offshore makes so much sense. It's a safety measure as well as a potential profit center.

The mainstream media have frankly done a lousy job of informing U.S. residents about the economic miracle happening on the opposite side of the globe. The emergence of China is without a doubt the biggest economic story of the twenty-first century. What do the United States's powerful television networks report on? Pandas. With a few notable exceptions, most newspapers have also missed the boat on China.

The speed of economic, social, and physical change in China is nothing short of breathtaking. Many China experts openly admit that after a few years away from major cities like Shanghai, Shenzhen, and Beijing, they often become disoriented when they return. The pace of change is so great that the skylines of China's cities can become almost unrecognizable after even a brief absence. I see amazing changes every time I return on my regular investment tours.

With so much change underway and so little attention being paid to it by the West, it's no small wonder there are many misconceptions about China. I want to introduce you to the new China, a dynamic and dramatically expanding economic superpower. I want to offer you the perspective and insight of an investment professional who is personally witnessing and participating in an unprecedented economic revolution. As an investor, I believe you also need to become familiar with the remarkable nature of the world's fastest-growing major economy. As the saying goes about so many things in China, especially about ideas and technologies derived from the West, this is capitalism with *Chinese characteristics*. I will explain the Chinese investment revolution as simply as possible, but I'm going to include a lot of supporting detail.

I do believe that it's important to understand the booming economic sectors we will be investing in as new China stockholders. Always keep in mind: China is still in transition from a centrally planned communist system to a free market economy. The rules are different from those anywhere else in the world and investors need to know how the system functions. That's why you'll find detail in this book about subjects that go beyond the day-to-day functioning of the markets.

In a transitional economy like China's, the government is always a factor and there are several levels of government that have a vested interest in the fate of many corporations. Sometimes, the Chinese government is industry's greatest friend. Sometimes, official policy discriminates, boosting investments in some companies while holding back other corporations in the same sector. The state is often a part owner or a majority owner of some of the nation's largest companies. Knowing the difference is vital to the success of your China portfolio. That's why I make it a point of pride to maintain offices inside China as well as in the United States.

China's two internal stock markets are a world unto themselves. I don't recommend investing a penny directly in either the Shanghai or Shenzhen exchanges. In fact, it is relatively difficult to do so. That's a good thing. Chinese regulators are doing their best to calm things down, but the two exchanges are wildly volatile. Stocks listed on the mainland are usually overpriced compared to stocks in the same companies traded in New York or Hong Kong.

I say it's easier, safer, and cheaper to stick to trading on U.S. exchanges.

What should investors do when stock trading in Shanghai and Shenzhen goes through one of its periodic frenzies? The cardinal rule is: Don't overreact. Don't go on a buying spree when Shanghai catches a dose of *share fever* and drives stock prices through the roof. And don't panic when China's internal markets fall back to earth.

Keep your eyes on the fundamentals, which I explain later in this book. You need to know how to take advantage of volatility. Sharp market setbacks have presented my subscribers with jaw-dropping buying opportunities. Sometimes, roaring markets in the throes of share fever are nothing more than a bright, flashing sell signal. To borrow a phrase, you need to know when to hold them and when to fold them.

I should reveal my bias before you go any further. Yes, I am very excited about the opportunities in China. I do believe there is a lot of money to be made by participating in the development of the world's fastest-growing major economy. But I am no zealot. The rising economic tide in China will not lift all boats. Profits are not guaranteed. Investors need guidance to discern the difference between winners, risky bets, and outright losers.

Yes, China presents us with an entirely new economic paradigm. We will be talking about millions, billions, and trillions of dollars circulating through a once-stagnant communist economy. Staggering amounts of new wealth are now being created. But this is not the time to ignite another dotcom frenzy. Quite the opposite.

I am, and always have been, a value investor. That means I look for companies that are underpriced. As a certified public accountant, I believe in examining the books. I want to invest in companies that have attractive financial metrics, not pie-in-the-sky promises for the future.

Join me as we explore the real-life economic miracle of China. Let me show you the investment opportunities available in the rise of the greatest economic power since the United States' emergence as an industrial giant during the twentieth century. Join me as we profit from China's capitalist revolution.

Dedicated to your profits,

Jim Trippon
Shanghai, China

PART I

TRENDS

WHY THE FUTURE BELONGS TO CHINA

CHAPTER 1

Sunrise in the East

CHINA BECOMES THE NEW WORLD SUPERPOWER

Success depends upon previous preparation, and without such preparation there is sure to be failure.

—Confucius

Wake up, world! China will have the world's largest economy within 10 years. That's a bold statement, but it's nevertheless absolutely true.

China's capitalist revolution officially started with a speech given three decades ago by the self-proclaimed supreme leader Deng Xiaoping. At the time, China's state-run economy was such a disaster that the government couldn't even feed its own people. Peasants were starving in the countryside.

Yet, for most Chinese people, the nation's decrepit state-run economy was the only system they had ever known. How could Deng Xiaoping drag China out of the economic dark ages and bring prosperity to the people . . . or at least provide enough food to fill their stomachs?

The year was 1978. A dramatic decision had been made in Beijing. China would scrap the communist principles that underpinned its economy and embrace U.S.-style capitalism. In his speech announcing this historic change of course, the supreme leader admitted China faced some serious economic problems. Then he said something utterly unexpected to kick-start the wheels of change in China:

"To get rich is glorious!"

Coming from the leader at the pinnacle of China's Marxist-Leninist communist economy, Deng's proclamation was truly astounding. From a politician of lesser stature, those few words would have been political heresy and a likely shortcut to a death sentence.

But Deng didn't stop there. He went on to say that some people and some regions of the country would be allowed to get rich first. Chairman Mao would have turned in his grave if he had heard such a statement. Mao, the late Chinese ruler, had spent more than a quarter of a century in a determined effort to destroy the inequalities of the nation's political and economic elites. But instead of creating a nation of equals, the old China resulted in the world's largest social and economic disaster.

Now, less than two years after Mao's death, his successor, the new supreme leader, was calling for a different revolution . . . a *capitalist* revolution in the world's largest communist country! Long before Mikhail Gorbachev prodded the Soviet Union into *perestroika* and ultimate oblivion, Deng Xiaoping had realized that his nation needed a total industrial and economic transformation to prevent chaos and avoid the possible collapse of the Chinese state. He had to create an economic miracle.

To those who criticized Deng, his reply was quick and pragmatic. "Black cat, white cat, all that matters is that it can catch the mice," he said. With that simple, time-tested metaphor, China's new leader brusquely dismissed decades of Marxist-Leninist ideology. The most important things, he believed, were jobs and money to feed and house his destitute nation. If that meant some people got rich in the process, too bad for communist ideology. Deng was China's first new capitalist.

Who Wants to Be a Chinese Millionaire?

It is hard to grasp how far China has come in just three decades. Although it is still a communist country in name, China has created more than 300,000 millionaires[1] and 108 billionaires.[2] (If you include the billionaires who reside in Hong Kong, China has an amazing *150 billionaires . . . more billionaires than any country in the world except the United States.*) That old communist, Deng Xiaoping, has already been proven right. Getting gloriously rich has turned out to be a surprisingly real possibility in the new China.

China's new rich are becoming richer with unprecedented speed. In 1999, the *Hurun Report* ranked only 50 Chinese as being wealthy. During this time, the cutoff point to rank among the gloriously rich required a net worth of a mere $6 million.

Today, the list has been expanded to include an almost unbelievable 800 Chinese multimillionaires. What's more, the cutoff point on the new listing of China's wealthy class has been boosted to almost $100 million. Never before has so much personal wealth been created in just a short period of time. The survey quite rightly compares the booming Chinese economy and the nation's new economic landscape to the Industrial Revolution of the United Kingdom and the robber baron period of the United States, "when vast areas of the economy were wide open to be exploited by smart, ruthless and fast-moving entrepreneurs."[3] China's capitalist revolution is creating economic growth much faster and on a much larger scale than in either Britain or the United States.

Table 1.1 illustrates the extraordinary growth of wealth in China that took place in the twinkling of an eye—just eight years.

Table 1.1   Towering China Wealth

Year	Minimum Wealth to Qualify For China's "Rich List"	Number of People on List
1999	$6,000,000	50
2000	$42,000,000	50
2001	$60,000,000	100
2002	$84,000,000	100
2003	$110,000,000	100
2004	$150,000,000	100
2005	$60,000,000	400
2006	$100,000,000	500
2007	$105,000,000	800

Source: *Hurun Report*, hurun.net.

According to the *Hurun Report,* the 500 richest Chinese are now worth an average of 100,000,000 yuan, which is the equivalent of $276 million US!

The story of wealth creation in China is revealed in part by the sectors in which the nation's new rich have flourished. Table 1.2 demonstrates the sectors in which the Chinese have made their money.

As depicted in Table 1.2, the top of the heap for creating independent fortunes in China is in property development. Rupert Hoogewerf, CEO of the *Hurun Report,* says, "What stands China out from the rest of the world is that *China's entrepreneurs are all first generation.* There has been a revolution in China's attitude towards wealth." Indeed, many Chinese I have met are jealous of the new rich, but all aspire to become wealthy themselves. That's why millions of ordinary Chinese people open stock market accounts every year, driving the Shanghai and Shenzhen exchanges to record heights.

In the process of creating an entirely new wealthy class, China's burgeoning economy has transformed the countryside.

Table 1.2   Millionaires by Sector

Sector	Number of People	Percent in Sector
Property	220	24%
Manufacturing	205	22%
IT	73	8%
Healthcare	55	6%
Finance	47	5%
Services	44	5%
Iron and steel	41	4%
Retail	38	4%
Food and drink	36	4%
Energy	36	4%
Apparel	33	4%
Mining	31	3%
Chemicals	22	2%
Civil infrastructure	14	2%
Agriculture	12	1%
Oil and gas	9	1%
Media	6	1%

Source: *Hurun Report,* hurun.net.

Approximately 300 million desperately poor people have been lifted out of poverty. Moreover, the average person's income has been increased by 400 percent.[4]

Towering new cities have sprouted in empty fields to house China's growing middle class and their places of business. A never-ending flood of peasants are flocking into urban areas from the rural countryside in search of jobs and prosperity. This relocation movement is widely considered one of the greatest migrations in history and it is still going on. Although population estimates tend to be a bit unreliable, it is projected that 160 cities in China now have a population greater than one million. No other nation in the world has ever seen anything like it.

The Recipe for China's Urban Transformation and Economic Growth

Economic growth is the driver of China's urban transformation. From 1978 to 2006, the average growth of China's gross domestic product (GDP) has exceeded 9.6 percent every year[5] (see Table 1.3). The speed and steadiness of China's growth is unprecedented. So is the scale of this economic event, touching the lives of 1.3 billion people.

In 2006, China's economic growth rate was a world-beating 11.1 percent.[6] Compare that figure to the United States, which considers a 3 percent annual growth rate to be a sign of a thriving economy.

In labor-intensive industries, China has become the dominant manufacturer in the world. Chinese factories now make 70 percent of the world's toys, 60 percent of its bicycles, 50 percent of its shoes, and more than one-third of the world's luggage.[7] Among higher-technology products, China produces two-thirds of the world's photocopiers and microwave ovens, one-third of all DVD-ROM drives and desktop computers, and a quarter of the globe's TV sets and PDAs.[8]

It's no secret that Chinese factory workers earn an average of $5.00 a day or less.[9] For those who wonder when China's economic growth will run out of steam, the vast pool of available workers in the countryside provides a tangible answer. China will not run out of cheap labor anytime in the near future, not when hundreds of millions of people are waiting in line to take their place in China's growing and much-envied middle class.

Table 1.3   China's Trade with the World ($ billions)*

	1995	1996	1997	1998	1999	2000	2001	2002	2003	2004	2005	2006
Exports*	148.8	151.1	182.7	183.8	194.9	249.2	266.2	325.6	438.2	593.3	762	969.1
% Change	23	1.5	20.9	0.5	6.1	27.8	6.8	22.4	34.6	35.4	28.4	27.2
Imports	132.1	138.8	142.4	140.2	165.7	225.1	243.6	295.2	412.8	561.2	660	791.6
% Change	14.3	5.1	2.6	–1.5	18.2	35.8	8.2	21.2	39.8	36	17.6	20
Total	280.9	289.9	325.1	324	360.6	474.3	509.8	620.8	851	1,154.60	1,421.90	1,760.70
% Change	18.7	3.2	12.1	–0.4	11.3	31.5	7.5	21.8	37.1	35.7	23.2	23.8
Balance	16.7	12.3	40.3	43.5	29.2	24.1	22.5	30.4	25.5	32.1	102	177.5

*PRC exports reported on a FOB basis; imports on a CIF basis.
Source: PRC General Administration of Customs, *China's Customs Statistics*; and the National Bureau of Statistics.
Compiled by the US-China Business Council.

In China, workers cannot easily relocate from city to city to increase their salary because, under Chinese law, people are required to have a *hukou* to take a job in a city.[10] A hukou is an official pass that allows migrants to travel into a city. Some estimates, however, indicate that the Chinese labor pool includes a floating population of 100 million workers who are considered illegal immigrants. These laborers, who stream in from the countryside without a hukou, earn as little as a dollar a day.

Compare China's wage advantage to the United States, where ordinary factory workers earn an estimated $15 to $30 per hour and auto-workers can earn more than $50 per hour when benefits are included.

Critics blame the Chinese government for unfairly gaining a competitive advantage by manipulating its currency—that is, by keeping the Chinese yuan (also known as the *renminbi*) artificially cheap. Politicians in Washington accuse China of undervaluing its currency by as much as 40 percent, giving the nation's exports an unfair advantage over U.S. products. Turn on the evening news and you'll see a steady stream of pundits like Pat Buchanan and Lou Dobbs beat this drum. That's not enough of an advantage, of course, to make up for the huge wage disparity between the United States and China. There is much more to it than that.

The fact is, there are many, many countries around the world with rock-bottom labor costs, not just China. In the Far East, nations including Vietnam, the Philippines, Indonesia, and Bangladesh all vie hungrily for manufacturing jobs, offering labor at rates even lower than those offered by China.

As is evident by studying Mexico, an inexpensive and sometimes desperate labor force is no guarantee of economic growth. Despite its shared border, Mexico has fallen behind China as an exporter to the United States. The benefits of the North American Free Trade Agreement (NAFTA), physical proximity, and an abundant supply of cheap labor have not been enough to give Mexico an economic edge over China.

The main ingredient in China's stunning recipe for success is its cheap, determined, and highly dependable labor force. Here's another key to the Chinese economic miracle:

> China's workers are supported by a uniquely determined and well-organized government that is focused on one prime directive: to make the economy grow by any means possible.

China's highly motivated and organized workforce is supported by an equally motivated government. Beijing is actively building a vast, modern national infrastructure that has already succeeded in turning the once poverty-stricken nation into the world's factory floor. New roads, railways, airports, universities, and all of the tools that are required to build a modern economy are in place in the major cities and under construction throughout the country. This immense modernization project is part of a determined effort to make China a world leader and cement its place as an advanced society on the global stage. Beijing has no intention of losing its economic status to a lower-wage manufacturing nation. The United States serves as a sharp reminder of the importance of staying on the leading edge of infrastructure, education, and research and development.

From Rags to Riches

How has China grown to become the world's second largest trading nation, surpassing Germany and now challenging the United States?

To some degree, the credit goes to our old capitalist mentor, Deng Xiaoping. He did much more than proclaim a slogan about the glory of riches. He put his life and freedom at stake to create a modern economy in China. Even though he had been purged from government as a "capitalist roader" in 1966 and was put under house arrest 10 years later as a so-called *rightist,* Deng ultimately unleashed the capitalist spirit in China. Nationwide acceptance of capitalism is another key to China's growth.

By promoting a program called the "Four Modernizations," Deng set out to revamp agriculture, industry, science and technology, and education. In agriculture, Deng's reforms set farmers free economically by allowing them to keep the profits from crops they grew in excess of their government-mandated quotas. Markets suddenly appeared in thousands of villages as farmers sold their produce for cash. Private and collective enterprises appeared as peasants began manufacturing toys, fireworks, bricks, and clothing. Successful peasants became rich by Chinese standards and began building homes, sparking the creation of larger industries.

To help promote industry, Deng created special economic zones (SEZs) in the coastal provinces of Guangdong and Fujian. As he hoped, tax subsidies attracted Hong Kong's manufacturing tycoons, who set up large-scale manufacturing plants. The number of zones eventually multiplied and the program of tax incentives and grants was expanded, creating an industrial explosion along China's coastal regions. Meanwhile, moribund state-owned enterprises (SOEs) faced (for the first time) competition and the prospect of bankruptcy.

Science and technology in China had been severely disrupted by the Gang of Four's ill-conceived attack on the nation's schools and universities during the notorious Cultural Revolution. As part of the modernization effort, an emergency program was put in place to expand the education system. Admissions were allotted according to merit-based testing rather than by party affiliation.

In a remarkable display of pragmatism, hundreds of thousands of students were sent out of the country, even to the capitalist Mecca—the United States—in search of modern scientific and technical knowledge. They brought U.S. expertise and attitudes home with them. Today, Chinese universities turn out an estimated 352,000 engineers annually.[11]

The Market Opens

Deng Xiaoping also deserves substantial credit for legitimizing stock markets in China. While touring the special economic zone of Guangdong in 1992, Deng realized the power of capital investment. As he marveled at the economic boom underway in cities like Shenzhen, he responded to a question about equity markets. He said, in a famous quotation, "Are such things as securities and stock markets good or not? It is permitted to try them out, but it must be done in a *determined fashion.*"[12]

It was one of Deng's last major pronouncements, and it unleashed a flurry of capitalism at home and abroad. The issuing of shares and trading of stock had been tried out in a tentative and poorly organized way for many years before Deng exhorted the nation to proceed in a "determined fashion."

After Deng's 1992 declaration, China's would-be capitalists took full advantage of their new freedom to get rich by trading in a growing pool of equities, not all of them legitimate. Stock markets flourished in mainland China, taking investors on a wild and volatile ride. Companies and brokerages appeared, soared, and sometimes disappeared. The two markets in Shanghai and Shenzhen now offer more than 1,800 listings and valuations are still highly volatile, when compared to Western standards.

The China Securities Regulatory Commission is engaged in an ongoing effort to root out corruption and bring stability to the nation's internal stock markets following a number of scandals and multiyear market crashes. Although many shady companies and dishonest brokerages have been put out of business, Shanghai and Shenzhen continue to be unstable and immature markets, driven more by individual speculators than by experienced institutional investors. Fortunately, the two mainland markets remain mostly off-limits to most foreign investors. Only a few large offshore institutions are permitted to trade in Shanghai and Shenzhen under the title of Qualified Foreign Institutional Investors (QFII).

Why is the regulation of China's internal stock markets a fortunate situation for U.S. investors? Because China's best companies were first listed overseas in New York and in the special economic zone of Hong Kong. That gives U.S. investors easy access to the best China has to offer. We have more access to quality Chinese companies than the Chinese people themselves.

Less than a year after Deng's determined pronouncement in favor of stock markets, a leading carmaker known as Brilliance China Automotive (CBA) was listed on the New York Stock Exchange, raising just $80 million in its initial public offering (IPO). Brilliance was listed as an ADR, an American Depositary Receipt. An ADR is a form of equity that represents ownership in the shares of a foreign company trading in U.S. financial markets, including the New York Stock Exchange and the NASDAQ.

Although U.S. investors were slow to warm up to ADRs from China, informed Chinese investors knew what a good deal the U.S. investment community was getting. Desperate for foreign capital, the Chinese government had listed only its so-called *National Champions* on overseas markets. Companies that earned the name National Champions included the biggest and most prestigious companies in the country, including vast state-owned enterprises that were undergoing capitalist reforms. To the frustration of China's would-be investors and the operators of the Shanghai and Shenzhen stock markets, the nation's biggest companies were not initially listed on mainland markets and some are still not.

Adr.com currently displays a total of 203 Chinese companies listed on U.S. exchanges (including Hong Kong–based firms).

Taking into account the Greater China region, another 108 Taiwanese firms are listed in the United States as ADRs. Many of the smaller, more speculative Chinese firms are listed on the NASDAQ. But the National Champions have emerged among the biggest firms on the NYSE by market cap. Five of the world's biggest companies (as measured by market capitalization) are now Chinese, compared to only three in the United States.

China's big five are China Life (LFC), PetroChina (PTR), China Mobile (CHL), Industrial and Commercial Bank of China (ICBC), and China Petroleum and Chemical (Sinopec) (SNP). The three U.S. firms still in the top 10 by market cap are ExxonMobil, General Electric, and Microsoft. Royal Dutch Shell of the Netherlands and Russia's Gazprom round out the list. (*Note:* Industrial and Commercial Bank is not listed in the United States.)

Chinese IPOs, especially those of Chinese banks floated on the Hong Kong market in 2007, have now joined the ranks of the largest IPOs in history. And Guangdong, the site of one of Deng Xiaoping's first special economic zones, has become the breeding ground for the greatest number of China's new millionaires.[13]

Expat Export Advantage

But there is much more to China's lightning-fast emergence as an economic superpower than the actions of one determined leader. China also had the advantage of an important base of knowledge and capital in Hong Kong, which had become a world financial and manufacturing capital during 155 years of British rule.

Advanced technical knowledge is being transferred from Taiwan, the breakaway Chinese province that had rebelled against the mainland in a sharp rejection of the communist revolution of Chairman Mao. As a free market economy, the island of Taiwan has become a world center for semiconductor manufacturing and a major investor in developing Chinese technology industries despite ongoing hostility between the two powers' governments. Expatriate Chinese communities in Singapore and Malaysia also contribute to China's emergence as a dynamically expanding economy.

The capitalist world has never seen anything like China's sudden economic expansion. The restructuring of the nation's economy and the resulting efficiency gains have contributed to a more than *tenfold* increase in GDP since 1978.[14]

Table 1.4   China's Top Imports 2006 ($ billion)*

Commodity Description	Volume	% Change*
Electrical machinery and equipment	219.0	25.3
Power generation equipment	109.2	13.4
Mineral fuel and oil	89.1	39.0
Optics and medical equipment	58.8	17.8
Plastics and articles thereof	37.8	13.6
Inorganic and organic chemicals	36.1	10.1
Ores, slag, and ash	32.2	23.6
Iron and steel	27.0	−15.4
Copper and articles thereof	17.2	33.3
Vehicles other than railway	17.0	38.4

*Percent change over 2005.
Source: PRC General Administration of Customs, China's Customs Statistics.
Compiled by the US-China Business Council.

Table 1.5   China's Top Exports 2006 ($ billion)*

Commodity Description	Volume	% Change*
Electrical machinery and equipment	227.4	32.0
Power generation equipment	186.6	24.7
Apparel	88.6	34.5
Iron and steel	51.9	52.2
Optics and medical equipment	32.6	28.0
Furniture	28.0	25.0
Inorganic and organic chemicals	23.2	21.5
Toys and games	22.6	18.4
Vehicles other than railway	22.4	34.8
Plastics and articles thereof	22.2	25.0

*Percent change over 2005.
Source: PRC General Administration of Customs, China's Customs Statistics.
Compiled by the US-China Business Council.

Exports are booming at an accelerating rate. China's trade surplus for the first six months of 2007 zoomed to a record $112.5 billion. The scale of China's expansion is so large that the statistics defy comprehension. For the month of June 2007 alone, exports were up by a breathtaking 85 percent over the previous year.[15] The nation's growth rate topped a stunning 11.9 percent that quarter. China's imports are also booming and would be headline news if exports weren't growing even more quickly (see Tables 1.4 and 1.5, respectively).

The Essential Consumer Class

The Chinese people are also beginning to embrace the new consumer culture. Retail sales are increasing at a rate of almost 18 percent per year, with total consumption for 2007 reaching above one trillion dollars.[16] The world's fastest-growing exporter is now the world's fastest-growing consumer market.

Newly wealthy Chinese consumers are snapping up automobiles and housing at record rates. Car sales rose by more than 34 percent in the first five months of 2007, despite an increase in taxes. House sales leapt by 27 percent in the same period, even though prices continued to climb.

One sure sign that people are feeling rich is an increase in travel, tourism, and dining out. Once again, the Chinese are posting sales increases in this luxury segment that would make any Western nation envious. Retail sales in lodging and catering rose by almost 19 percent in the first five months of 2007 to hit a new high of $12 billion. According to a report by the Credit Suisse bank, China's booming economy will boost it to second place behind the United States as the world's biggest consumer market by 2015.

China's appetite for the better things in life can sometimes seem surprising, considering that a recent survey[17] revealed that the average income for urban workers in Beijing was less than $4,600. The driving force behind the surge for luxury items is the capital's top wage earners who report much better earnings. High-level workers in the banking, securities, legal services, and petroleum exploration industries earned an average of $12,500 in 2006, a princely sum, considering the purchasing power of a dollar or its equivalent in Chinese yuan.

The Chinese Academy of Social Sciences conducted a three-year study and reported that as many as 240 million people have now joined the ranks of the nation's middle class. Just two decades ago, a mere eight million Chinese households were considered middle class. The academy defines the middle class as managers, professionals, skilled technicians, and service workers who earn between $2,500 to $10,000 a year.[18] There is still a great deal of room for growth. China won't be fully transformed from an agricultural society into an industrial economy before the year 2015, possibly not until 2021.[19] That is not all that far away.

In real terms, the income of China's middle class has grown faster than even Deng Xiaoping might have hoped when he first exhorted the nation to go ahead and get rich. The per capita income of urban residents rose from a miniscule 343 yuan (about $44) back in 1978, to an average of 11,759 yuan in 2006. The per capita income of farmers stood at 134 yuan in 1978 (about $17), growing to 3,587 yuan in 2006[20] (about $473, adjusted for inflation). Farmers still lag city dwellers by a wide margin, but millions have at least been lifted above starvation wages.

Who are these new Chinese? The blue uniform of Chairman Mao is long gone. So is the angry image of dissent in Tian'anmen Square. The Chinese middle class is now much like any other in the world: white collar, college-educated, and ambitious. Unemployment is still high, approaching 10 percent, and so the level of competition for a good job is fierce. Competition for jobs means workers tend to remain stable once they have found a position.

The government is scrambling to create new industries and new jobs for the millions of educated young people and migrant farmers who enter the workforce every year. Always worried about the specter of social unrest, the Chinese government has set itself the mind-boggling task of creating 10 million new jobs every year.

Because China enjoys a household savings rate of at least 30 percent,[21] the potential to invest China's capital pool in new industry and to expand internal consumption is still enormous. The nation's growing pool of wealth is transforming China's internal economy, and these changes influence our investment decisions.

A study by Grey Global Group of Beijing found that the members of the younger generation in China are very confident about their futures and driven to get ahead in the business world. Money and self-image are important to this new breed of Chinese consumer. They are willing to experiment by buying new gadgets and wearing trendy clothes. More than half say they need to take risks to be successful, and Grey Global interprets this finding as the emergence of a huge unmet demand for new trends from consumer product companies.[22]

As disposable income increases, we expect to see the pool of Internet subscribers within China to grow substantially. It is projected to reach 200 million by the end of the decade and may pass that milestone much sooner. We also expect the market for appliances, especially luxury appliances, to increase. And there is little doubt that demand for automobiles, oil, energy, cell phones, and housing will continue to rise exponentially as millions of Chinese migrate to the major cities and join the nation's capitalist revolution.

Rising Economy, Hidden Dragon

The statistics we read in the newspaper can be misleading in a country as large and diverse as China because they paper over the wide gap between urban wealth and rural poverty. On a national basis, China's gross domestic product (GDP) per capita was a relatively humble $1,800 in early 2007.[23] The average worker's income is expected to rise to $2,400 by 2010.[24] But this surprisingly low measure of individual wealth and productivity is distorted by the huge number of Chinese people who live in the countryside, many of them yearning for an opportunity to enjoy the prosperity of city dwellers. The World Bank estimates that 150 million Chinese still live in absolute poverty without adequate food or clothing.[25] But the Bank says the lot of the rural Chinese is improving, with an astounding 400 million people having been lifted out of poverty between 1985 and 2001.

A word of advice: Investors should always look at China's growth statistics with a jaded eye, but not because they tend to be overstated, as was usually the case with centrally planned economies like the now defunct Soviet Union. To the contrary, China's numbers are usually understated. Why? Because China prefers not to alarm the world or attract undue hostility from its trading partners with revelations about the scale of its economic expansion. As the always-quotable Deng Xiaoping once said, "China should disguise its ambition."

Here's a startling example. In early 2006, the Chinese government decided to take a deeper look at its recent economic growth statistics and concluded it had made an error, a very big one. Beijing bureaucrats suddenly discovered (or perhaps revealed) that the size of the economy had been underestimated by a whopping $280 billion. *That's billion, with a capital "B."* The revelation of China's new growth figures touched off the equivalent of an earthquake on the world's economic scene.

Many comfortable assumptions were shaken up badly. Observers in the European Union noted with particular alarm that China had suddenly replaced Italy as the world's sixth-largest economy. Europolitix.com worried aloud, "The Asian dragon now threatens the French number five ranking." Of course, both France and Italy have now been left in the dust by China's economic dragon.

Just how important was this discovery? The revision of China's 2006 economic growth estimates followed a one-year economic census that discovered the missing $280 billion in hidden economic output during 2005. To put it in perspective, the census result meant that China had discovered a new internal economy equal in size to the economies of entire countries. This previously unrecorded economy is on a par with the economies of Turkey or Indonesia.

The new economic numbers boosted China's gross domestic product for 2005 to almost $2 trillion, as measured by the conventional yardstick of nominal GDP (see Figure 1.1). That resulted in a colossal jump of 17 percent in the GDP from the previous year.

The new GDP numbers transformed our own understanding of the Chinese economy, and they made it a much more attractive investment arena. Previously, statistics were calculated from data provided by institutions such as large factories, a method left over from the days of the centrally planned communist economy. In China's increasingly market-based economy, these supply-side figures entirely missed the cash component of economic activity.

Supply-side economic numbers fail to take into account the amount of money that consumers *actually spend*. This ongoing accounting error has thoroughly distorted perceptions of the Chinese economy for decades and given economists countless sleepless nights. The new numbers reveal a picture of China that is far more balanced and hopeful than we had dared imagine. What has been revealed is a giant service economy within China. North Americans take the service economy for granted because so much of our economic activity is based on value-added services and knowledge-based products. It turns out that China is also fast becoming a player in this arena.

Fears that the Chinese economy was in a bubble, driven largely by excessive investment, have been eased considerably. This shows that the national economy is much more diversified and healthier than anyone had known.

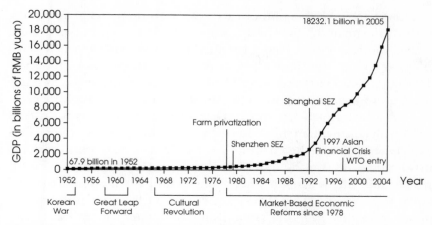

Figure 1.1 People's Republic of China's Nominal Gross Domestic Product (GDP) from 1952 to 2005
Source: billcara.com.

There may be more hidden economic activity to be revealed in China, adding to its already phenomenal growth profile. Dong Tao of Credit Suisse First Boston says that China may still be underestimating the size of its service sector by another $200 billion.

Who Is the World's Real Economic Superpower?

The shape of the world economy is changing so quickly that it will soon be unrecognizable to those who are not following the China story. It may seem that China still has a long way to go before it eclipses the United States's economy, which had a GDP of more than $13 trillion in 2006.[26] But the day is coming.

Conventional wisdom predicts that China will overtake the United States in 2035 in nominal GDP terms. But that prediction severely underestimates China's accelerating economic growth and the scale of its economic transformation.

The World Bank has an alternative and very credible way of measuring national economic output, the PPP method: *Purchasing Power Parity*. Many economists believe that PPP provides a more meaningful way of comparing economies than the usual nominal GDP figure. Here's what the World Bank figures tell us. As measured by Purchasing Power Parity, the Chinese economy is *already* the second largest on the planet, following only the United States.

This is a big shift in America's worldview and it calls for a few words of clarification. Purchasing Power Parity is a way of comparing the economies of countries without the distortions caused by currency exchange rates and other disparities. Rather than estimating GDP by national currencies, PPP calculations compare the average costs of goods and services between countries. Imagine, for example, that a factory worker in China has to pay much less for a new washing machine than his counterpart in the United States. The Chinese worker may be earning less than the U.S. worker in absolute dollar terms, but he may be richer than the raw numbers indicate because of his greater purchasing power for a given basket of goods and services. The World Bank and the Central Intelligence Agency (CIA) use PPP when comparing national economies.

By the standard of Purchasing Power Parity (PPP), China had a GDP of *$10.1 trillion* in 2006.[27] Compare that with America's GDP, estimated at $13.13 trillion, using the same PPP yardstick. China is very close and catching up quickly.

As I said at the beginning of this chapter, China is definitely on track at current growth rates to surpass the United States as the world's number one economic power within 10 years. In its "Eleventh Five-Year Plan, 2006–2010" the Chinese government set ambitious goals to transform the nation into a "well-off society" in the next 20 years and to *double* GDP in 10 years.[28]

China's growth affects the whole world and it has been a particular boon to its Asian neighbors. Roughly one-third of China's trade volume is conducted within the Asian region, amounting to approximately half a trillion dollars. This increased trade volume has allowed Asian nations to enjoy higher rates of growth than industrialized countries in the West.[29] Japan is one of the great beneficiaries of increased trade with China. The island nation is finally reporting GDP growth of more than 2.5 percent after years of stagnation, when growth barely touched the 1 percent mark.

Former Australian prime minister Paul Keating calls China the motor of the world economy.[30] Keating, who has also served as Australia's treasurer, calculates that China adds $400 billion to $500 billion worth of new wealth to the world's economy every year, an amount that has now surpassed the U.S. contribution to global wealth creation.

In Table 1.6, you'll notice that the United States ranks number one among China's trading partners. The United States' exports to

Table 1.6   China's Top Trading Partners, 2006 ($ billion)*

Rank	Country/Region	Volume	% Change*
1	United States	262.7	24.2
2	Japan	207.4	12.5
3	Hong Kong	166.2	21.6
4	South Korea	134.3	20.0
5	Taiwan	107.8	18.2
6	Germany	78.2	23.6
7	Singapore	40.9	23.3
8	Malaysia	37.1	20.9
9	The Netherlands	34.5	19.8
10	Russia	33.4	14.7

*Percent change over 2005.
Source: PRC General Administration of Customs, China's Customs Statistics.
Compiled by the US-China Business Council.

Table 1.7   China's Top Suppliers, 2006 ($ billion)*

Rank	Country/Region	Volume	% Change*
1	Japan	115.7	15.2
2	South Korea	89.8	16.9
3	Taiwan	87.1	16.6
4	United States	59.2	21.8
5	Germany	37.9	23.3
6	Malaysia	23.6	17.3
7	Australia	19.3	19.3
8	Thailand	18.0	28.4
9	Russia	17.7	37.3
10	Singapore	17.7	7.0

*Percent change over 2005.
Source: PRC General Administration of Customs, China's Customs Statistics.
Compiled by the US-China Business Council. All rights reserved.

China are rising very quickly, up an average of 22 percent a year since China joined the World Trade Organization in 2006,[31] contributing to the sustained prosperity of the United States. And, while the United States may not be number one among countries exporting to China, the trend is still positive (see Table 1.7).

China's Biggest Import: Your Factories

One of the great mistakes made by U.S. politicians and television commentators is to focus angrily and exclusively on the downside of China's ballooning export surplus. But why blame China?

Here are the facts. Many of the factories that have been built in China in the past decade are the result of offshoring. Unlike outsourcing, offshoring involves the shifting of an entire corporation's production apparatus to the Chinese mainland to take advantage of low labor costs. According to Ma Kai, the minister of the powerful National Development and Reform Commission, China has received more foreign direct investments than any other country for 14 straight years. By the end of 2006, there were 590,000 foreign-invested firms in China.[32] This is unlike any economic event in history. More than half a million foreign firms have staked their place in China. Tens of thousands have uprooted their factories and voted with their feet by rebuilding manufacturing facilities inside China!

This is an astonishing economic migration. It is clear that the Chinese economic miracle has as much to do with offshoring by developed nations and foreign investment as any initiative sponsored by the Chinese. China's entry into the World Trade Organization in 2001 may have given foreign businesses comfort that they could operate in a stable legal structure. It was foreign firms, however, many of them Asian as well as from the United States, that are responsible for a massive shift of production facilities to China's mainland.

The consequences of the Chinese offshoring revolution are effectively a double-edged sword. Stephen Roach at Morgan Stanley estimates that more than half of America's whopping trade deficit with China results from offshore production.[33] Millions of U.S. workers have lost factory jobs to offshoring. Yet America's unemployment rate remains remarkably low. Clearly our economy is creating new jobs to fill the gap. What's more, economists at Morgan Stanley estimate that cheap imports from China have saved U.S. consumers $600 billion since the mid-1990s and provided a source of cheap parts to U.S. manufacturers.

The rise of Chinese consumerism may eventually begin to reduce the yawning trade imbalance that has struck so much fear into the hearts of U.S. economists. Chinese authorities acknowledge that their economy is far too dependent on exports. That's why news of increasing Chinese retail consumption and the development of an internal service economy is music to the ears of economic observers inside China and outside.

China's leaders want to build an economy that won't suddenly collapse if foreign demand for their exports begins to wane. As one Chinese diplomat told *The Economist,* "Imports, that's real diplomacy, because it means you're attractive to others. It means that other countries need you, not that you need them."[34]

By the same token, developed economies, the United States in particular, all desperately want China to consume more foreign goods and services. Thanks to China's ballooning trade surplus, it has become the world's largest holder of foreign exchange reserves. In a stunning development, China passed the one trillion dollar mark in foreign exchange holdings during the last quarter of 2006.

As if a trillion dollars of extra cash weren't enough, the flood of foreign currency continues to pour in at an accelerating rate. During the first half of 2007, another quarter of a trillion dollars was added to the nation's pool of foreign reserves.[35]

This unprecedented trove of wealth gives China immense power. Until 2006, most of China's foreign exchange surplus was simply invested in U.S. Treasuries and bonds issued by other industrialized nations. As every investor knows, U.S. Treasuries may be secure, but they do not pay a princely return.

When China passed the trillion dollar mark in foreign exchange assets, banking authorities decided they needed a better return on their holdings. Two hundred billion dollars has been carved out of the nation's foreign exchange reserve to invest in securities that offer higher returns and higher potential risk. How the Chinese decide to invest this block of money is the big question.

Interestingly, the first slice of China's foreign exchange, $3 billion, was invested in the private capital firm Blackstone. That money was rushed into the market to take a stake of the company before it launched its IPO. The remaining billions have the power to shake up stock markets. How ironic it is that a nation still run by the Communist Party has suddenly acquired the financial resources to reshape the world's capital markets. (As 2007 came to a close, Beijing decided to allocate a significant portion of this fund to bailing out ailing banks and to the provision of badly needed social services.)

Chinese tariffs and government-sanctioned protectionism are often blamed for the nation's huge trade imbalance with the United States. But that is far from the truth. China is actually twice as open to trade as the United States is and three times as open as Japan. According to C. Fred Bergsten, the highly respected director of the Peterson Institute for International Economics, China has been the fastest-growing market for U.S. exports for the last 15 years. Testifying before the Senate Finance Committee, Bergsten pointed out that U.S. exports to China grew by 160 percent between 2000 and 2005, while America's exports to the rest of the world rose by only 10 percent. China's ratio of imports to GDP has soared from 5 percent in 1978 to 30 percent in 2005.[36]

The United States is unlikely to become competitive with Chinese labor costs in the foreseeable future. That's why the United States must invent new services and knowledge-based products that will appeal to China's growing middle class.

Wise Words from the Guru

The United States remains a powerful innovator. China, however, has the potential to become a much bigger customer for U.S. innovation and become a powerful partner with our knowledge-based industries. Because China has a population of 1.3 billion people, we have not yet begun to experience its full potential. China is still at an early stage of development compared with the growth curve of other countries, including Japan, South Korea, and Taiwan. According to Carsten Holz, a professor of economics at Hong Kong University of Science and Technology, these countries all experienced a similar economic rise from poverty. Judging by the track records of Japan, South Korea, and Taiwan, it appears that China still has a lot of room to grow. Holz predicts that China's GDP (measured by purchasing power) will surpass the United States in 2010 and says it will continue growing rapidly until 2015.[37]

Because of China's economic transformation, the world is entering a new phase of economic development that will shake up every assumption about our world that has prevailed for the past century. There is simply no doubt that China will emerge as the world's largest economy. But China cannot achieve this goal without ongoing capitalist reform and investment.

As an unabashed capitalist, I see the emergence of China as an opportunity for investment. As an investor, I expect the Chinese economy to continue growing and I look forward to seeing my clients' and readers' investment dollars grow right along with them. I, for one, believe that nothing helps economies grow like enlightened capitalism. And, nothing returns profits to investors like well-informed capitalism.

The most populous country in the world is still in transition from communism to free market capitalism. As investors, you and I have the privilege of profiting from China's new capitalist revolution.

CHAPTER 2

Sunset in the West

THE END OF U.S. ECONOMIC SUPREMACY

*What is of the greatest importance in war is extraordinary speed:
One cannot afford to neglect opportunity.*

—Sun Tzu

My dad was an infantry soldier during World War II. If you saw the movie *Saving Private Ryan,* you would have a good idea of what landing in Normandy was like for my dad and his comrades on the early morning of D-Day. Of the 550 men in Dad's engineering battalion, only 50 were still alive after the first hour of combat. This certainly became a defining moment in the life of my dad.

Likewise for the millions of U.S. soldiers who spent World War II fighting in the Pacific, the war years were a defining experience not only in their personal lives, but for their entire generation. When Dad and his fellow soldiers came home from the war, they returned to a United States that was much stronger and more prosperous than the one they had left.

At war's end, the United States was the world's only remaining and functional industrial power. Europe was, for the most part, a bombed-out shell, with Germany, France, and the Soviet Union all in shambles economically. Japan, likewise, was made to pay a devastating price for initiating what the Chinese still refer to as the "War of Japanese Aggression."

Unlike Europe and Japan, however, the United States was full of shining new factories that could produce abundant quantities of industrial and consumer products with great speed and efficiency. Hence, the world's industrial center of gravity had shifted to the United States from Europe for the first time in history. The United States became the world's leading economy and its primary manufacturing center. We continued to hold the position as the world's largest economy throughout the remainder of the twentieth century and into the twenty-first.

A Tough Pill to Swallow

This will be a tough pill for many of us to swallow, but the fall of U.S. economic and military supremacy is inevitable, and will be here much sooner than most of us realize.

It has happened to every empire throughout history. In ancient times, the Persians and the Medes ruled the world. Later, the Greeks and Romans took center stage. The British Empire in the nineteenth century was the economic and military superpower that governed much of the planet. It appears, unfortunately, we are next on this list of Great Power nations to go into eclipse.

The question for investors is brutally simple:

> Will we go down with the ship? Or will we seize upon new opportunities and prosper?

The simple fact is that the United States is exporting its money *and* its manufacturing muscle to China at a rate that is both alarming and unprecedented in this nation's history. During 2006, the United States rang up a stunning $232.5 billion trade deficit with China. In fact, the United States is running a multibillion-dollar trade deficit with every one of its top 10 trading partners.[1]

While the United States continues its headlong plunge into deepening trade deficits, China has been accelerating in exactly the opposite direction, ringing up unprecedented surpluses. During the first half of 2007, China's trade surplus zoomed to a record-breaking $112.5 billion. That was the first time the nation's surplus broke through the 100-billion dollar barrier over any six-month period. While the United States' deficits grew deeper, the Chinese trade surplus had skyrocketed by 85 percent over the previous year for the month of June 2007.[2] Sadly, it seems the United States is driving in reverse.

It may seem like a distant memory, but the United States was the world's banker less than 20 years ago. It is now the largest debtor nation that the world has ever seen. The U.S. debt-to-GDP ratio is a mind-boggling 400 percent.[3] While Chinese wage earners save more than 30 percent of their income, the United States has descended into a negative personal savings rate. Despite their empty bank accounts, U.S. consumers continue to flock to malls and big box stores, buying cheap imports, financed by credit cards and by loans made against the evaporating equity they hold in their homes. The cyclone of volatility that rattled the world's equity and credit markets following the United States' notorious subprime loan debacle revealed all too sharply the wobbly underpinnings of the U.S. economy.

China now holds the power. What's more, the bulk of China's financial power is poised directly over the United States' economy. As I mentioned in the first chapter, China cashed in most of its foreign currency surplus by purchasing U.S. Treasury bonds until recently. In other words, China routinely accepted U.S. IOUs in return for its huge reserves of foreign exchange.

The tide began to turn when the Chinese central bank announced it would diversify its holdings into higher-yielding assets, having realized that Treasuries just didn't pay enough interest compared to other investments. Because U.S. Treasuries are denominated in a sinking currency, the U.S. dollar, China's returns have been depressed even further.

But China's decision to diversify a portion of its investments is just a hint of the economic threat the United States faces. The Chinese government has the option of simply turning off the flow of credit to the United States entirely by declining to buy any more U.S. Treasuries. The result would be a sudden rise in U.S. interest rates, which would trigger a steep plunge in the value of the dollar and a bloodbath on U.S. stock markets. The net effect would be a deep recession in the United States, so deep that it might well rival the Great Depression of the twentieth century.

Would China ever pull the plug on the U.S. economy? Most experts say that would never happen because the deliberate devastation of the United States' economic engine would severely damage the Chinese economy as well. We are, after all, their best customer.

That argument sounded convincing until recently. As the drumbeats of anti-China rhetoric and trade protectionism rose once again in Washington, China threw down the gauntlet in what was called the "nuclear option."

Xia Bin, the finance chief at China's Development Research Center, warned in early August of 2007 that China could sell its U.S. dollar holdings if Washington imposed trade sanctions to force a revaluation of the Chinese yuan. Another high-ranking official, He Fan, of the Chinese Academy of Social Sciences, went even further, declaring that Beijing had the power to set off a dollar collapse if it chose to do so.[4] Beijing has the power because it holds an estimated $900 billion worth of U.S. Treasury notes, bonds, and other assets, all denominated in dollars. The exact amount is a state secret. Kathy Lien, chief strategist at dailyfx.com warned, "With $1.3 trillion in foreign reserves, most of which are held in U.S. dollars, China has what it takes to cripple the U.S. economy."[5] Since she made her remarks, China's foreign exchange reserves have risen to approximately $1.5 trillion and Chinese clout on the world economic scene has increased proportionally.

U.S. citizens are witnessing an eerie echo of the nuclear standoff that made the Cold War with the Soviet Union so terrifying. Under a doctrine called *Mutually Assured Destruction* (MAD), the United States and the Soviets stockpiled enough weapons to obliterate each other several times over. If either side launched a first strike, the other could be sure that the attacker would certainly be annihilated in return. MAD was a powerful incentive for both sides to be very cautious in word and deed. Neither was foolish enough to launch a first strike.

Throwing caution to the wind, U.S. politicians are now becoming increasingly belligerent toward Beijing despite the obvious vulnerability of the U.S. economy. Before invoking the "nuclear option" in August of 2007, Chinese authorities had never so much as warned that they might stop *buying* U.S. Treasuries. But as anti-Chinese rhetoric rose in Washington, Beijing upped the ante, threatening to crush the U.S. dollar, the world's reserve currency, with a massive sale. In their view, sweeping trade sanctions by Washington would be the equivalent of a "first strike." A full-scale counterattack would be justifiable.

Without question, such a move would have devastating economic global consequences. Of course, China would also suffer grievously if it pulled the trigger in this game of *Mutually Assured Economic Destruction*. But the mere fact that Beijing issued the threat speaks volumes about the new balance of power in the world.

The United States has suddenly become an economic weakling. It, unfortunately, grows ever weaker as it continues to pile up mountains of new debt with China and with its many other trading partners.

The Game of Mutually Assured Economic Destruction: Will China Pull the Trigger?

While the United States' economic underpinnings erode, China is quickly becoming the world's dominant economic power, one with a very aggressive temperament. But why would China play such a dangerous game of brinksmanship with Washington? Would it actually pull the trigger?

The answer to that crucial question requires some understanding of the Chinese psyche. Most Westerners, unfortunately, have little knowledge or appreciation of China's proud new mentality. China's grueling hardships in the past remain a mystery to most U.S. citizens. The important fact is this: *China does not want to be seen as a threat, but it will not tolerate being threatened. Not after what has happened in its past.*

Over the course of 2,000 years, China has historically reigned as one of the world's greatest economic powers and an early scientific pioneer. It is responsible for earthshaking inventions that include the creation of gunpowder and paper. During its long history, China regarded itself as the world's most advanced civilization, having created sophisticated systems of government, law, and banking. The country's own name, China, translates literally into the phrase "The Middle Kingdom." In other words, the Chinese look upon their nation as being the center of the world.

Unlike other great civilizations of the past, the ancient Chinese did not conduct wars of conquest to create a sprawling empire. Instead, neighboring countries, including Korea and Japan, adopted many key elements of Chinese civilization, including systems of writing, the arts, and law. As China's culture spread, so did the nation's trade in exotic exports such as silk and fine porcelain, products that would eventually be prized in every corner of the world.

Among Westerners, Marco Polo may have been one of the first to appreciate China's power and its economic potential. During his travels in the eleventh century to a city that would eventually become known as Beijing, the Italian explorer marveled at China's enormous wealth, its complex social structure, and its developed industries—including the manufacture of steel and the mining of coal, which he called "the rock that burns." Commerce was conducted with paper money, yet another Chinese invention. Marco Polo's elaborate and grand descriptions of Kublai Khan's Imperial Court shaped European understanding of China for centuries to come.

The West now has a much different perspective, one shaped by events that the Chinese would consider quite recent. Since the eighteenth century, many Europeans and U.S. citizens have looked down on China as an economic backwater and a political basket case. Torn by civil wars, invasions, famine, and ruinous political purges like the Cultural Revolution (1966–1976), China has been an object of pity, perhaps even scorn. While the United States was experiencing its own emergence as an economic superpower, it employed legions of so-called Chinese coolies to perform hard labor, including building the nation's railroads. Convinced of their own manifest destiny, many U.S. citizens thought of China as a helpless giant, unable to feed its own people or move out of the Middle Ages.

But modern Chinese people have an entirely different view of history, and they remain intensely proud of ancient China. They look back upon the nineteenth and twentieth centuries, the years before the nation's economic resurgence, as "the hundred years of humiliation." They blame foreigners for the decline of the Middle Kingdom, and not without justification.

The Century of Humiliation

Britain's two Opium Wars against China during the nineteenth century resulted in some of the worst humiliations. China lost both wars and was forced to legalize British-sponsored opium imports from India. Untold numbers of Chinese people became addicts as a result. French troops supported Britain in the second Opium War. As a result of that conflict, China was forced to yield Hong Kong to Britain and to open several ports to trade under the terms of grossly unfair treaties. Several countries followed Britain and forced unequal terms of trade onto China. British meddling in China also sparked several rebellions, leading ultimately to the collapse of the Qing dynasty in 1911. The ancient Chinese system of government never recovered from these blows. Fatally weakened, China was left prone to brutal civil wars and foreign invasions.

Japan invaded China twice, once in the nineteenth century and again during the twentieth century. Bent on expanding the Japanese empire and exploiting Chinese raw materials and markets, Japanese forces invaded the province of Manchuria in 1931. Ongoing conflicts ultimately provoked full-scale war between the two nations in 1937. Japanese forces responded brutally to Chinese resistance with a policy called "The Three Alls": kill all, loot all, burn all. The horrors and documented atrocities of the Japanese occupation continued until the end of the Second World War. Although Japan had been defeated, postwar China was weak, demoralized, and wide open to a communist takeover.

How deep do the wounds from history's humiliations go? To this day, the Chinese government issues angry diatribes whenever the Japanese prime minister visits the Yasukuni war shrine in Tokyo. The shrine is revered by the Japanese because it honors 2.5 million soldiers who have died since 1869 fighting for Japan. But the shrine is a direct affront to Chinese sensibilities because it houses fourteen Class A war criminals, some of whom were implicated in the atrocities in China.[6] Japan says the annual visits to the shrine are intended to pray for peace, not to honor war criminals, but such diplomatic insults still provoke angry anti-Japanese demonstrations in China's major cities.

The details of Chinese history may seem unimportant and irrelevant to Western businessmen and investors. But the sharp contrast between China's rich imperial past and its most recent hardships form a 2,000-year-old backdrop that shapes the nation's state of mind and its political actions to this day.

There is little evidence that Chinese leaders or its people accept any national responsibility for their century of humiliation. Foreign meddling is to blame. They feel intensely that the hundred years preceding the nation's current economic revival were an embarrassing deviation from the nation's long history as the world's most advanced civilization. The Chinese leadership is intensely focused on the goal of reestablishing the nation's position as the world's preeminent power.

"You're Either With Us, or Against Us"

Few Westerners understand why China has a chip on its shoulder, why it responds so angrily to U.S. complaints about unfair trade practices. But to be lectured by politicians from the United States, a rich and powerful nation that didn't even exist a few hundred years ago, is seen by virtually all Chinese people as unbearably insulting. Even though China is already on a trajectory to become an economic superpower, the nation's leaders remain acutely aware of the horrors of the past and worry about the impoverished millions of peasants still eking out a living in rural areas. Any threat to China's current economic rise, especially from a wealthy Western nation, is regarded as utterly intolerable by Beijing.

It is true that Beijing may not always be a fair player in the game of economic competition. Complaints about rampant and open piracy of Western intellectual property are never effectively addressed. China's currency may indeed be unfairly undervalued compared with the U.S. dollar, but the Chinese point to other Asian nations that may be equally guilty of currency manipulation, but are not criticized by the United States.

China sees the world in terms that were immortalized by President George W. Bush when he said, "Nations are either with us or against us." By the same token, China does not make fine distinctions among competing nations. Beijing reserves particular suspicion and animosity for the nations it holds responsible for its 100 years of humiliation.

Growing the Chinese economy is a concern that trumps all others. Beijing is determined that there will be no going back. That is why Chinese authorities hinted they might be prepared to "go nuclear" economically if the United States were to fire the first shot in a trade war. For Chinese officials, Mutually Assured Economic Destruction is preferable to humiliation.

For the record, President George W. Bush scoffed at the idea of an attack on U.S. currency, saying it would be "foolhardy." U.S. Treasury Secretary Henry Paulson said the idea was "absurd."[7] Indeed, several days after Chinese officials threatened a run on the dollar, a posting appeared on the central government's main web site saying, "U.S. dollars and government bonds are an important part of China's foreign reserve investments." Those words were attributed to an unnamed official with the People's Bank of China.[8] Although the threat had officially been withdrawn, China had sent a powerful message to the highest levels of the U.S. government. With one verbal shot across Washington's bow, Beijing exposed a fundamental weakness of the U.S. economy.

As One Country Rises, Another Country Falls

It gives me no pleasure to predict a rocky road ahead for the United States' economic supremacy. But the evidence of danger to the U.S. stock market and the nation's economy is plain to see and should be a concern to all U.S. investors.

Call me a lone voice in the wilderness if you wish. But remember, no politicians and very few financial analysts or media pundits have predicted major economic reverses in the past. Even the biggest events, including the Great Depression, the Asian financial crisis of the 1990s, and the market crash that followed the dotcom debacle, were not predicted by those who should have seen the warning signs. (To be fair, one newspaper, *Barron's*, sounded the alarm before the "tech wreck" of 2001–2002, but most market analysts were too busy issuing buy recommendations to say anything negative about the United States' much-heralded "new economy").

I'm as patriotic as any U.S. citizen and that's why it's my reluctant responsibility to issue some words of caution about the direction we're now headed in. Prudent investors need to know where the dangers lie *before* another crisis erupts, not after.

In my view, the United States is staring helplessly at a double-barreled economic shotgun. Both barrels are aimed directly at our nation's economic heart. Even more appalling, we U.S. citizens are facing a danger that we created ourselves.

The United States is running *two* massive and extremely dangerous deficits, not just one. First, there is our current account deficit, which reflects the United States' profligate spending abroad relative to our income from imports. During 2006, the current account deficit ballooned to $811 billion. The net U.S. foreign debt rose to the almost incomprehensible level of more than $2.5 trillion.[9] *That's trillion, with a capital "T."*

Believe it or not, some economists declared those figures to be good news when they were revealed in 2007. Why? Because the United States' total foreign debt actually turned out to be lower than they had expected. It seems foreign governments, including the Chinese and private investors, saved our bacon that year by purchasing almost two trillion dollars worth of U.S. securities. But this is economic quicksand.

If the dollar continues to decline, returns to foreign investors from U.S. securities will drop right along with them. We are in danger of a fire sale of U.S. stocks, bonds, and currency, and we have little left in the way of reserves to deal with a crisis. Our current account deficit is draining both our credibility and our credit as a trading nation.

The U.S. government has not responded to the current account imbalance despite repeated warnings that the situation is becoming dangerous. Until relatively recently, it was believed that a current account deficit of more than 3 percent of any nation's GDP was unsustainable. Alarmingly, the United States' deficit for the first quarter of 2007 rose to 5.7 percent. It averaged 6.5 percent of GDP during 2006.[10]

The United States simply cannot be expected to continue to build up foreign liabilities forever. The economic equivalent of a perpetual motion machine or an antigravity device does not exist. According to a study by a think tank called the McKinsey Global Institute, a 30 percent depreciation of the U.S. dollar may be required to eliminate the current account deficit.[11]

Just as serious as our foreign debt is the United States' parallel deficit, that is, the federal government's budgetary shortfall. The official U.S. budget deficit during 2006 was a walloping $248 billion. That's bad enough, but it would have been far worse if corporate accounting standards had been used. An analysis by *USA Today* found that the federal government would have racked up a $1.3 trillion loss for the year if generally accepted accounting principles had been used.

Ordinary accounting requires corporations as well as state and local governments to count expenses as soon as a transaction occurs, even if payment is to be made later. But the federal government doesn't follow these rules and its obligations for Social Security and Medicare don't show up on the books. The newspaper concluded that taxpayers are on the hook for an astronomical $59 trillion, more than $500,000 for every household in the country.[12]

These are truly frightening figures, but are they manageable? The United States would have to generate an astonishing amount of new wealth from burgeoning export industries to finance its obligations. The government would have to raise far more revenues from a prosperous workforce that would somehow be growing wealthier by the year. Unfortunately, that's not happening. The trends are not in our favor.

"A country cannot close its trade deficit if its economy is being moved offshore," says Paul Craig Roberts, a former assistant secretary of the treasury for economic policy.[13] Roberts points out quite accurately that moving U.S. production offshore hits the trade deficit from both ends because when goods once produced domestically become imports, the nation's ability to export consequently declines. So much for the idea of burgeoning export income.

What about growing wealth in the workforce? The evidence indicates that the United States' displaced workers are highly unlikely to be moving to better-paying jobs or earning wages that might enrich the nation's tax base. The Bureau of Labor Statistics says the nation's 10 fastest-growing job categories are: home health aides, network systems and data communications analysts, medical assistants, physician assistants, computer software engineers, physical therapist assistants, dental hygienists, dental assistants, and personal and home care aides.[14] If the Department of Labor is correct, the prospects for a rich export economy based on an expanding knowledge-based industrial sector are not bright.

Sending U.S. jobs offshore may also be damaging the U.S. economy more than official statistics reveal. A detailed analysis by *BusinessWeek* magazine found that offshoring by U.S. firms tends to create a phantom gross domestic product. If so, official calculations about the size of the United States' GDP are off by about $66 billion and the United States' growth rate is lower than Washington is telling us.

China, in the meanwhile, continues to grow stronger as it spreads both its economic and political influence throughout Asia and the developing world. The effect of Chinese economic growth and demand for resources has been especially profound on an old U.S. ally, Australia. In the years before Deng Xiaoping launched China on the capitalist road, Chinese trade with Australia amounted to no more than $100 million a year. In 2006, trade between the two nations had soared to $33 billion, making China Australia's largest trading partner.[15] As a supplier of resources, especially liquid natural gas (LNG), and as the world's largest source of uranium, Australia is looking forward to an increasingly close and profitable relationship with its Chinese customers.

This Australian trend is appearing throughout the Asia-Pacific region. China is now, or soon will become, the primary trading partner for all countries in East Asia, replacing both Japan and the United States, according to a report from Australia's prestigious Lowy Institute.[16] In fact, Chinese trade with the whole of East Asia soared above the half-trillion-dollar mark during 2006.

As the volume of trade in the region continued to grow at a double-digit pace year after year, China racked up a trade *deficit* of $87.5 billion in 2006 with its East Asian trading partners. Exporting nations were only too happy to increase their shipments and rake in more than $87 billion worth of income.

China has now become the largest export market for the Republic of Korea, the number two export market for Japan, the number three export market for Thailand, and the number four export market for Indonesia, Singapore, the Philippines, and Malaysia.[17]

As China's industrial engine grows in strength, its appetite for raw materials and commodities has become voracious. The country represents about 5 percent of the global economy, but it consumes a whopping 20 percent of global aluminum and copper production, about 30 percent of steel, iron ore, and coal, and a remarkable 45 percent of cement produced annually. China's increased commodity consumption has also been a boon to Latin American countries, including Chile, Argentina, and Brazil, which have joined in the export of raw materials to fuel the Chinese economic engine.[18]

Losing the Race

Although Beijing was once hostile and openly antagonistic to capitalist economies and to U.S. allies in Asia, the new China is now leveraging its economic clout in a much more productive and friendly fashion. Chinese diplomats are working feverishly to weave a web of positive ambassadorial and trading relationships with neighboring nations throughout Asia. A total of 28 countries and regions, which account for a quarter of China's foreign trade, have joined the Middle Kingdom's ever-expanding free trade territory. Eleven free trade zones have either been set up already or are currently being negotiated with China's trading partners.[19] While the United States tries to expand its free trading relationships beyond Mexico into the developing nations of South America, China is aggressively staking out its territory among the world's fastest-growing economies in Asia.

The United States' traditional allies in the Asia-Pacific basin are, unfortunately, feeling snubbed by the United States at a time when Beijing is actively courting them. In a recent incident, key Asian leaders had hoped to revive relations with the United States by staging a celebration in the form of an official summit. The summit was scheduled to mark 30 years of official ties between Washington and ASEAN, a group representing the rapidly growing nations of Brunei, Darussalam, Cambodia, Indonesia, Laos, Malaysia, Myanmar, the Philippines, Singapore, Thailand, and Vietnam. Unfortunately, President Bush canceled his planned celebration of Asian-American cooperation in the summer of 2007 because of the intense pressure of events stemming from the war in Iraq.

Adding to the region's feeling of isolation from the United States, U.S. Secretary of State Condoleezza Rice also canceled her planned meeting with the much larger 27-member ASEAN Regional Forum (ARF) in Manila. The ARF is the only high-level official security group in the Asia-Pacific region, and it includes Russia, India, China, and the European Union.[20] It marked the second time Rice dropped out of the Asian summit in three years. Walter Lohman, director of the Asian studies center at the Washington-based Heritage Foundation, called the situation a significant setback in U.S.-ASEAN relations, noting that ASEAN is the largest U.S. export market after Europe and Japan. Rice was forced to bail out because of the worsening conflict between the Palestinians and the Israelis.

In September of 2007, President Bush did manage to put in an abbreviated one-day appearance at the Asia-Pacific Economic Cooperation (APEC) summit of Asia-Pacific economies in Sydney, Australia. Unfortunately, he managed to alienate many of the economic leaders, while Chinese president Hu Jintao struck a chord with the assembled summit. President Hu talked about the economic benefits that Asian nations are gaining from Chinese trade. President Bush focused on the threat of terrorism, referring to the summit as OPEC instead of APEC, and mistakenly calling his hosts Austrians instead of Australians. The slight did not go unnoticed. Even Bush supporters in Australia were offended, saying the president's comments illustrated "the increasing tin ear of the Bush administration in Asia."[21]

As the United States turns its attention away from the Asia-Pacific region, China is extending its reach in all directions. In addition to establishing multiple free trade agreements, it is opening diplomatic channels and courting influential groups, including ASEAN + 3 (the extra three are Japan, South Korea, and China itself).

According to the Business Roundtable, China's ambitious expansion of its free trade zones puts the United States to shame.[22] The organization says, "China, a new entrant to the world trading system, has pivoted off of its 2001 entry into the WTO [World Trade Organization] to launch an active FTA [free trade] diplomacy, with negotiations involving 28 countries underway or proposed, including a partially completed agreement with ASEAN, negotiations with the Gulf Cooperation Council, Australia, New Zealand, Pakistan, and the South African Customs Union." The United States is negotiating with just seven trading partners.

The Business Roundtable is sharply critical of U.S. inaction on trading relationships around the world. The organization's stinging report is entitled, "We Can't Stand Still: The Race for International Competitiveness." We appear to be losing that race.

The report notes that when a free trade agreement is concluded that excludes the United States, "U.S. exporters suffer trade discrimination; they face higher tariffs than their competitors, as well as more limited access to services markets. . . . This discrimination is particularly significant where U.S. businesses are trying to gain a competitive foothold in key strategic markets. The result of a lack of agreements is weaker positioning in the global economy." It goes on to say that "Approximately 300 FTAs have been negotiated around the world, with more in the offing; the United States has implemented only ten. Our major international competitors are not standing still. Neither should the United States."[23]

Ambitious Chinese trade negotiators have definitely not been standing still when it comes to relations with central Asia. China opened a new Asian diplomatic and economic channel with its oil-rich (widely ignored) neighbors by creating the Shanghai Cooperation

Organization (SCO). The group includes Kazakhstan, Kyrgyzstan, Tajikistan, Uzbekistan, and Russia. SCO is considered a competitor to NATO.

Chinese authorities have also been careful to establish friendly economic and diplomatic relations with Africa, a continent that is hungry for outside assistance and attention. Although China's growing influence in Africa has received scant notice in the United States, Chinese leaders, including President Hu Jintao and Premier Wen Jiabao, have made several high-profile state visits to the continent. Among the countries they have paid their respects to are: Morocco, Nigeria, Kenya, Egypt, Gabon, Algeria, Ghana, the Republic of Congo, Angola, South Africa, Tanzania, and Uganda. China's remarkable diplomatic push has not gone unappreciated among African leaders and their people. China scored surprisingly well in an opinion poll conducted by the Pew Global Attitudes Project in 2007. The Pew researchers found that among 8 out of 10 African nations surveyed, China was named among the country's closest allies. Of course, the United States has poured billions of dollars worth of aid into Africa over the course of many decades, but China, a relative newcomer to the continent, rivals the United States in all but one country (see Figure 2.1).[24]

Although Chinese trade with Africa is relatively meager, less than $38 billion during 2005, China has promoted friendly relations by sponsoring approximately 900 aid projects on the continent.[25] China has much to gain by establishing solid relations with Africa's 53 nations. Chief among its interests is oil, and China has endured severe international criticism for assisting in the development of the oil industry in Sudan, a country that has become an international pariah for its genocidal policies in Darfur. Other natural resources, including aluminum ore, bauxite, are abundant in Africa. These natural resources will become very important to China's future industrial expansion.

Also, more than 800 Chinese companies have set up shop in Africa to build telephone networks, extend railroads, and establish satellite communications systems.[26] The teeming African populace also has the potential to become a very large market for inexpensive Chinese manufactured products. Without question, the continent is becoming an integral part of the Chinese sphere of geopolitical influence, while the United States remains preoccupied elsewhere.

	Closest Allies	%	Biggest Threats	%
Ethiopia	U.S.	58	Eritrea	86
	China	53	Nigeria	69
	EU	40	al Qaeda	29
Ghana	U.S.	65	al Qaeda	33
	Britain	56	Ivory Coast	15
	China	32	Nigeria	14
Ivory Coast	China	69	France	68
	U.S.	69	B. Faso	60
	S. Africa	37	Mali	23
Kenya	U.S.	63	Somalia	55
	China	41	Sudan	33
	Britain	28	al Qaeda	32
Mali	U.S.	56	al Qaeda	31
	China	49	U.S.	15
	France	48	Ivory Coast	12
Nigeria	U.S.	58	U.S.	32
	Britain	40	Iran	14
	China	27	China	12
Senegal	France	50	U.S.	15
	U.S.	45	Gambia	12
	China	30	al Qaeda	8
S. Africa	U.S.	57	Zimbabwe	41
	Britain	37	Nigeria	26
	EU	25	Iran	19
Tanzania	U.S.	37	al Qaeda	27
	China	32	U.S.	23
	Britain	22	Iran	13
Uganda	U.S.	57	Sudan	42
	Britain	29	Somalia	21
	Kenya	24	DRC*	17

*Democratic Republic of Congo

Figure 2.1 Allies and Threats in Africa
Source: Pew Global Attitudes Project.

The Defensive Military

As China extends a seemingly friendly hand of diplomacy around the globe, it continues to build a modern and lethal military force. Once a large, but poorly trained and ill-equipped army of more than a million troops, the newest version of the People's Liberation Army (PLA) threatens to obliterate the United States' claim to be the world's lone superpower. It has acquired advanced weaponry, international reach, and the ability to fight a modern, information-based war. China has been accused of numerous cyberattacks on governments and financial institutions in the United States and the United Kingdom.

China's military spending is shrouded in secrecy and the Pentagon believes that Beijing's public statements about its military are deliberately misleading. On March 4, 2007, Beijing announced a 17.8 percent increase in its military budget, bringing its official defense budget estimate for 2007 to approximately $45 billion. But the Pentagon says actual Chinese defense expenditures remain far higher than the officially disclosed figures.

In its 2007 report, "Military Power of the People's Republic of China," the U.S. Department of Defense says China's pub-lished defense budget does not include major spending programs that include the cost of strategic forces, foreign arms purchases, research and development, and paramilitary forces. Contrasting with China's lowball budget, the Defense Intelligence Agency (DIA) estimates China's total military spending for 2007 could be between $85 billion and $125 billion.[27] The highest estimate listed in the Pentagon report puts Beijing's military spending above $140 billion on a purchasing parity power basis.

Beijing prefers to portray its military expenditures as purely defensive, but the Chinese arsenal is vast and could be used in a war of aggression. The PLA already is among the most powerful armed forces in the world and it continues to grow exponentially. Few U.S. citizens appreciate the fact that China has an array of nuclear-tipped intercontinental ballistic missiles (ICBMs) capable of strik-ing any target in the continental United States. In fact, China's ICBM arsenal is currently being modernized with new missiles to increase their survivability in case of a nuclear attack.

The People's Liberation Army has not grown significantly in numbers over the years, with a standing force remaining at approxi-mately 1.4 million troops, but the armaments at the disposal of PLA soldiers have increased in both potency and in numbers. China is building a blue-water navy, armed with 5 nuclear subma-rines, 53 diesel submarines, and more than 100 destroyers, frigates, and missile patrol aircraft. A new type of nuclear-powered ballistic missile submarine equipped with sea-launched ICBMs is currently undergoing sea trials. There are also unconfirmed reports that an aircraft carrier may be under construction.

The Chinese coast is bristling with hundreds of short-range ballistic missiles, while the navy's ships are armed with supersonic cruise missiles, antiaircraft missiles, and precision-guided missiles designed to destroy targets on shore or at sea. In the air, China has an arsenal of more than 1,500 fighters and almost 800 bombers. In space, China has 35 satellites. China stunned the aerospace community in January of 2007 by scoring a direct hit on one of its own obsolete weather satellites, demonstrating the army's ability to knock enemy spacecraft out of the sky.[28]

Many PLA armaments were purchased from Russia, but the Chinese are not content with the quality of weapons acquired abroad, especially Russian fighter aircraft. China is building an aircraft industry of its own to assemble both commercial and military airplanes. Because it has been blocked from purchasing strategically important components in Western nations, China is conducting an active espionage program to acquire secret weapons technologies.

Military officials in Beijing are also acutely aware of the importance of information management in combat. The Pentagon believes they have developed the capability to severely disrupt U.S. communications and Internet systems. But Beijing has no intention of challenging the United States directly with its growing military power, at least not yet. The Chinese are cagey enough to realize that direct military competition with the United States was largely responsible for the collapse of the Soviet Union.

The Chinese have focused on two goals in the near term. Above all, Beijing is intent on defending its deeply held claim to sovereignty over the island of Taiwan. The last time the Taiwanese angered Beijing with a seemingly insignificant diplomatic faux pas, in 1995, the Chinese army quickly fired 10 missiles into the waters off Taiwanese shores. The United States responded by sending two aircraft carrier groups into the region to enforce its commitment to stability in Taiwan. China backed down, but resented the United States' perceived interference in what it considers an internal affair.

Today, with its growing military power, China has not developed the ability to launch an attack against the U.S. military, but it has definitely upped the ante over Taiwan. Any future showdown between the U.S. navy and Chinese forces in the Taiwan Strait would be a bloody affair and it's likely the United States will take pains to avoid another confrontation with China's new navy and its potent missile arsenal. In military parlance, the Chinese have greatly "upped the cost" of enforcing the United States' commitment to oversee a peaceful resolution of the dispute over Taiwan.

For the time being, China and the rest of Southeast Asia are content to let the U.S. military do the costly work of maintaining regional stability in the Asia-Pacific region, using the enormous contingent of U.S. forces already positioned there. But every Asian nation is well aware of China's growing military power and political influence.

When North Korea stunned the world by testing a nuclear weapon on October 6, 2006, the United States' response was uncharacteristically muted. Washington relied on Beijing to apply pressure on North Korean dictator Kim Jong-Il. The tactic worked. Six months later, North Korea announced that it would agree to shut down its main nuclear facility after $25 million in previously frozen funds were transferred to Pyongyang from a bank in Beijing.

The question remains: Why is China expanding its military power so aggressively if its intentions are purely defensive? In August of 2007, U.S. Navy Secretary Donald C. Winter posed that very question during a visit to Australia. Winter said that China must be more transparent about its military intentions and its naval build-up in the Asia-Pacific region. As the navy secretary said, "We continue to take a look at China and try to understand what the Chinese intent is. . . . We're trying to understand not only what it is that they're doing, but why they are doing it."[29] Some observers say the Pentagon is worried that China is preparing to deal with future internal unrest and economic difficulties by stimulating nationalist fervor by using aggressive military and diplomatic tactics.[30]

But China is also building its military muscle to enforce its great power status. According to the U.S. Defense Department, China's leaders see the first two decades of this century as a "twenty-year period of opportunity," believing that conditions will be peaceful and conducive to economic, diplomatic, and military development. This period of peace will quietly enable China's rise to become a great power. The Pentagon says China is conducting its "peaceful development" campaign to soothe foreign concerns over China's military modernization and its global agenda by proclaiming that

China's rise will be benign.[31] All the while, China continues to extend its military reach.

After the 20-year period of opportunity, China's tone may change dramatically as it comes into competition with the United States over the world's dwindling oil supplies. China's oil imports are increasing with breathtaking speed as automobile owner-ship soars, a worrisome trend at a time when the nation's existing petroleum reserves are drying up. Almost 60 percent of China's oil imports already come from the Middle East and that proportion is going to increase. By 2015, China will look to the Persian Gulf for at least 70 percent of its oil supply.[32]

Chinese oil companies have attempted to diversify the nation's petroleum supplies by buying access to reserves in Kazakhstan, Russia, Venezuela, Sudan, West Africa, Iran, and Canada, but there is simply not enough oil available from these sources to slake China's growing thirst. By 2030, China may have more cars than the United States and import just as much oil as the United States does today.[33] Its need for oil is certain to spark competition for energy supplies, particularly oil, with the world's biggest and most profligate energy user, the United States.

The People's Liberation Army is currently very much aware that China depends on the United States navy to patrol the sea lanes through which most of the nation's oil imports from the Middle East are shipped. This fact alone gives the U.S. effective control of oil in the event of a showdown over supplies. That is a prospect that China cannot passively accept.

Ninety percent of China's oil is currently transported by tankers through the narrow and strategically vulnerable Straits of Malacca. Most of this oceangoing oil originates in the Persian Gulf, and Chinese authorities are deeply uncomfortable that the U.S. navy has effectively assumed responsibility for ensuring the continuity of China's oil shipments through the Gulf and another potential choke point at the mouth of the Gulf, the Straits of Hormuz.

Looking forward two or three decades into the future, U.S. and Chinese officials understand fully that Middle Eastern oil will become increasingly scarce while Chinese demand continues to grow. Worldwide competition for precious oil will inevitably become more intense. The potential for open conflict or at least a peaceful superpower showdown is certain to increase, and the Chinese have no intention of leaving themselves vulnerable to U.S. intimidation or dominance.

That's why the Chinese have been busy courting Saudi Arabia, Iran, and oil-rich central Asian nations, while building a formidable blue-water navy. Continued economic expansion is simply not negotiable, and Beijing's mandarins are well aware that the nation's economy already depends on imported oil. Future oil shipments are a lifeline that the world's emerging superpower is preparing to defend aggressively.

Will it come to a war over oil? I certainly hope not. But the Chinese are not ignoring the possibility. Will the dollar collapse under pressure from China? Again, I hope not, but we are currently undermining the economic foundation of the United States and leaving ourselves vulnerable to foreign attack. Will U.S. influence in Asia be eliminated? Probably not, but it is in decline as the United States closes military bases in Uzbekistan and Kyrgyzstan under increasing pressure from China and Russia through the Shanghai Cooperation Organization, an expanding and aggressive rival to NATO.[34]

U.S. investors can no longer count on the world remaining their oyster forever. Whether China achieves all of its ambitions, there is no doubt that the Middle Kingdom is determined to regain its status as a world superpower, both economically and militarily.

By China's own reckoning, it is only halfway along the road to full industrialization. The nation's planners expect to complete the process in the year 2021,[35] remarkably close to the end of the much-heralded 20-year period of opportunity. But China does not see its long-term future solely as the so-called workshop of the world. While economic planners push the nation's industrial expansion into remote and underdeveloped regions in the West, a more sophisticated initiative is well underway in China's heavily industrialized eastern coastal area.

Why China Needs Its Own Neil Armstrong

Chinese leaders have long wished to develop an advanced technological infrastructure supporting a modern, knowledge-based economy. In other words, they wish to compete with the United States and Europe on the cutting edge. As you will read later in this book, China is building an auto industry that aims to overwhelm the likes of Toyota and General Motors. It is building a banking system that already houses the world's largest financial institutions (as measured by market capitalization). China has skipped a generation in the construction of a modern communications system by moving directly to a massive system of wireless telephony without the expense of constructing a national grid.

Looking into the future, the Chinese are building an aircraft industry that hopes to compete with Boeing and Airbus in the construction of commercial aircraft. China is also building sophisticated weaponry including missiles, guided bombs, rockets, naval craft, and a range of military aircraft, including fighters, bombers, transports, trainers, and reconnaissance aircraft.

China ultimately has its sights set on the moon and Mars. In 2003, China became the third nation in history to put a man into space. The China National Space Administration plans to put a man on the moon in 2024, and expects to begin unmanned missions to Mars as early as 2014. China's existing space program has already launched satellites for foreign customers and placed many of its own vehicles in orbit. There is little doubt that some Chinese spacecraft are designed for military applications.

For decades, China has been underestimated as a potential economic competitor because of its lack of innovation, and not without reason. The Chinese are justly notorious for their failure to protect Western intellectual property from piracy. China has been able to appropriate Western technological discoveries without payment or penalty, but that is a practice that cuts both ways. By failing to develop homegrown technologies and intellectual property, China has also failed to build knowledge-based industries that can develop original and competitive ideas. By permitting the theft of intellectual property, the Chinese state has also undermined domestic industries that might have benefited economically from innovation. There is little incentive to create a culture of innovation if any new idea can be routinely copied free of charge.

Chinese authorities are belatedly attempting to come to grips with the problem. In 2006, research and development budgets grew by 22 percent, but the nation's R&D totals are still far behind those of the United States, both in real terms and as a percentage of gross national product.[36]

Remarkably, China rose to become the third-highest-ranking country for patent applications in 2007. China is now ahead of the European Union but still behind the United States and Japan as measured by the total number of patent applications filed. Chinese industry has experienced a 32 percent surge in patent applications since 2005.

As China strives to build a knowledge-based economy, it has established industrial parks and welcomed the likes of Microsoft, General Motors, and IBM to establish facilities there. Cooperating with the Chinese has begun to pay off for Microsoft. The company spent 15 years and lost billions of dollars of revenue trying to sell its software at a profit in China. It was impossible to succeed when pirated Microsoft programs were being sold on the street for as little as three dollars.

After committing more than $100 million to new research within China, Microsoft's investments have begun to pay off. In 2006, the Chinese government required personal computer makers to load legal software onto their computers.[37] The relationship between Microsoft and China is now flourishing. Bill Gates enthuses about the quality of researchers working in his Chinese development centers. The Chinese president, Hu Jintao, made a point of visiting Microsoft headquarters in Seattle before meeting with President Bush on his visit to the United States in 2006. Microsoft products are being sold legally at a fraction of their price in U.S. markets, but Gates is optimistic that he has established the foundation for a profitable business in China.

In another example, IBM is shifting its focus to China as well. After selling its personal computer business to the Chinese firm Lenovo, IBM began moving some of its own operations to the Chinese mainland. IBM announced in the fall of 2006 that it would move its global procurement headquarters to Shenzhen. That marked the first time the headquarters of an IBM corporatewide organization had been located outside the United States. IBM's move reflects the growing shift of high technology to Asia. The company says it chose China for its procurement headquarters because it has nearly 3,000 suppliers across Asia, accounting for 30 percent of the $40 billion that IBM annually spends on procurement.[38]

Investors Beware . . . Time to Get Ready

There are many uncertainties surrounding China's ability to succeed in the creation of an advanced, knowledge-based economy. But there is little doubt that China will continue to grow rapidly and the world's industrial focus will continue to shift to the East for the foreseeable future. Investors cannot ignore this trend or its effect on U.S. corporations. Diversification abroad is just as important for the investment community as it is for the industries that began offshoring their factories many years ago.

Not surprisingly, it is Deng Xiaoping, the leader who implemented China's modernization, who set the standard for Chinese behavior during its current growth phrase. In the early 1990s, he gave a few words of guidance to China's foreign and security policy apparatus. These words have come to be known as the "24 character" strategy. Deng's words accurately describe China's strategy as it approaches its destiny as an economic and military superpower. They are as follows:

> Observe calmly; secure our position; cope with affairs calmly; hide our capacities and bide our time; be good at maintaining a low profile; and never claim leadership.

China will not bide its time quietly forever. One day, it will claim leadership. Investors beware, and get ready!

CHAPTER

3

Breaking the Chains of the Bicycle Kingdom

CHINA'S DREAMS COME TRUE

Nothing in life is to be feared. It is only to be understood.
—Madame Curie

Two clients of mine recently reminded me of the enormous gap in most U.S. citizens' understanding of the new China. Like many of my clients, this gentleman and his wife had been to Beijing and the Great Wall a few years after China opened itself up to Western tourism. Because they had never made a subsequent trip back to Beijing, they still retained their first impressions of China more than two decades later.

Remembering the Forbidden City, they recalled a particularly poignant scene. Near the exits, a large black automobile had been parked in the middle of a wide plaza with an ancient structure in the background. Just in front of the official-looking car was a photographer with a large, old-fashioned camera. He approached my two clients and asked them with a series of gestures if they would like to have their picture taken. Somewhat baffled, because they were carrying their own cameras, the two politely declined. Soon after, a large Chinese family in blue fatigues assembled to be photographed and it became clear that the centerpiece of the picture was to be the car, not the outskirts of the Forbidden City.

The image spoke volumes about the nation's economy and the hopes of the Chinese people not so very long ago. Beijing had almost no automobiles except for official, Soviet-style limousines. Despite the absence of automotive traffic, the city's wide boulevards were jammed with millions of bicycles carrying blue-suited men, women, and children toting their belongings through a gray haze created by coal-burning heaters and stoves in every home. The idea of owning a family car and a modern apartment was as far from reality for the average Beijing resident as the fantasy of buying a private jet is for working class U.S. workers. That's why they posed their families in front of this impossible luxury, a large family car, and paid a photographer a few yuan to capture a fantasy they could not even record because they had no camera of their own.

As they chatted about their memories of the old China, my clients called up a host of images that demonstrated just how far that country has come, and how little we in the West have noticed. While shopping in a grim, state-run department store, they found nothing at all that would be pleasing as a gift for friends and family back home. China offered few consumer luxuries beyond white silk handkerchiefs. When my two friends opened their shoulder bags to dig around for a camera they were swarmed by dozens of curious onlookers eager to see what consumer delights their Western visitors harbored in their portable treasure chests. (They carried emergency rations of peanut butter and cans of tuna, along with photographic gear and the usual assortment of travel paraphernalia like hats, scarves, and rain gear . . . nothing special, but a trove of wonders to the ill-fed, shabbily dressed but friendly mob that looked on.)

As you'll see in this chapter, China has changed far more than the West has. The strictures of communism have been abandoned, but China retains a heavy measure of state involvement in the economy. Historically a trading society and an international economic force, China has left behind the days of isolation and humiliation. The dream of building a business or owning shares in a corporation is no longer a forbidden fantasy. The Chinese people may have lost some of the security that went with cradle-to-grave socialism, but they have gained a measure of prosperity and hope that was the stuff of pure fantasy a remarkably short time ago . . . a time that my two clients remembered as if it were yesterday.

The New Frontier for Gucci, Rolex, and Mercedes-Benz

When most Westerners think about China, they still have a distorted and outdated mental picture. Many Americans still believe that China is populated by masses of impoverished people, dressed in Chairman Mao suits or People's Liberation Army uniforms, riding around Beijing in a sea of bicycles. That was true in the 1970s, but today's China is full of rapidly modernizing megacities with freshly poured streets and landscaped urban boulevards. Modern China is now a place where you are more likely to see a Mercedes-Benz or BMW than a bicycle.

As a result of this move toward luxury goods, the legendary "bicycle kingdom" of China has now been overwhelmed by traffic jams. China is the world's second-largest auto market, and cycling has become a dangerous venture on crowded, smoggy city streets. The newly mobile Chinese people are quickly indulging their dreams of luxury transportation. In fact, BMWs and Mercedes sales are rising more quickly in China than anywhere else in the world. Sales of the BMW brand, especially the China-made 5-Series sedans, rose 36 percent to 22,891 vehicles during the first half of 2007. Over roughly the same period, Mercedes-Benz sold 15,830 cars and SUVs in the Chinese market (including Hong Kong and Macau). That's up 30 percent from a year earlier.[1]

America may be losing its edge as a manufacturing base, but it is leading the charge in China's wealth explosion. The creation of brand consciousness in China has become a big money science, studied in depth every year at the China Luxury Summit in Shanghai. Hundreds of Western marketing experts and executives from top-tier brands gather in the ballrooms of Shanghai's posh Marriott Hotel to work out strategies to entice China's superrich consumers to indulge deeply in the fruits of materialism. Even the richest material fruits of all, private jets and oceangoing yachts, are on sale from the likes of Boeing Business Jets, Embraer Aircraft of Brazil, and Ferretti Yachts of Italy.

The Boston Consulting Group, Ernst & Young, and Goldman Sachs have been studying the emergence of the wealthy elite in China for years. According to some estimates, this privileged elite is growing by as much as 20 percent a year, putting China on track to become the second-largest luxury goods market in the world next to the United States by 2015. The China Market Research Group estimates that the volume of luxury goods sold in China will top $12 billion in the next decade.[2] The worldwide luxury goods market is currently estimated at $50 billion. The contrast to the old China could hardly be greater.

According to a report by Goldman Sachs, Chinese purchases of high-end items intended to display social status—including designer handbags, perfumes, and watches—will grow by 25 percent annually until 2009.

Poverty is still a serious problem in the countryside, but in China's gleaming first-tier cities, the drab ghost of China's past is quickly being pushed into the dark recesses of memory by the newly arrived spirits of Coco Chanel, Louis Vuitton, and Christian Dior. Every major luxury brand has a presence in cities like Shanghai and Beijing, just as they have for years in the capitalist bastions of Hong Kong and Taipei. For the ultra-wealthy Chinese, there are lavish events, such as the Millionaire Fair in Shanghai. Every year, it attracts hundreds of China's nouveau riche, who are eager to discover satisfying ways to spend their newfound wealth and enhance their prestige. Diamond-encrusted cell phones and multimillion-dollar Swiss watches now hold the same appeal to China's new rich as they do to the conspicuous consumers of the West.

As the level of wealth in China grows with the nation's booming economy, brightly lit shopping malls and luxury stores are beginning to spring up throughout China in second-tier cities such as Harbin, Wuxi, and Wuhan. These teeming urban areas, with a population greater than a million and names virtually unknown in the West, have become home to luxury brands like Giorgio Armani and Prada. Each of these brands has exactly 21 outlets in the new China.[3]

Fine watches have also become an increasingly important sign of success for Chinese men. In 2006, China rose to become Switzerland's tenth-largest export market as sales of fine Swiss watches grew more quickly than in the United States, Japan, Singapore, or any nation in the oil-rich Middle East. The Federation of the Swiss Watch Industry says $334 million worth of timepieces was sold in China in 2006, a 14.9 percent increase over the previous year.[4] The new China is the new luxury goods destination.

The Essential Expanding Class

Ultra-luxury consumption is only the tip of the iceberg. The emergence of a large middle class is also vital to the development of a stable society and a sustainable economy. Chinese Premier Wen Jiabao recently stressed the importance of developing a consumer mentality among the nation's burgeoning middle class. Premier Wen warned the nation that it was far too dependent on investment and exports, a problem that made the economy unstable because of its excess liquidity and its vulnerability to global downturns.

At first glance, China's consumption curve seems to be rising exponentially. In addition to the notorious traffic jams caused by swarms of new cars, cities like Beijing and Shanghai are surrounded by vast housing projects and dense clusters of freshly built apartment towers. But look inside these new homes and you will find the average Chinese family continues to live a relatively Spartan existence.

We have to adjust our perspective to understand the reality of China's newly affluent middle class. To qualify as a member of the middle class, a family must earn at least 80,000 yuan, or approximately $10,000 a year.[5] It doesn't sound like much, but it's enough to purchase a modest automobile and an apartment, a bonanza by the standards of a mere 30 years ago. Most members of the middle class are academics, doctors, engineers, office staff for state-owned enterprises, and bureaucrats.

You may remember the term *Purchasing Power Parity*, which I used when discussing China's gross national product. The fact that a middle-class family is able to purchase a car and a home on an income of 80,000 yuan a year indicates that a very small salary by U.S. standards goes a relatively long way in China. The Chinese equivalent of a $10,000 annual U.S. income gives a Chinese family the power to purchase a lifestyle that would cost many times that amount in any industrialized Western nation. This is a real-life demonstration of Purchasing Power Parity in today's China. In terms of hard currency, a middle class family may appear to be impoverished. But when measured by purchasing power, this same family is beginning to approach parity with an average Western family.

Although the members of this emerging class own homes and automobiles, they are generally considered conspicuous savers, not consumers by the standards of most Western economies. Although the new middle class family typically splurges on a television, a washing machine, and a few small appliances, various estimates indicate that the Chinese people save between 30 percent and 40 percent of their income, a great deal more than their Western counterparts. Chinese families know they must save because government pensions and health insurance plans, once provided by state-run enterprises, are now largely a thing of the past.

Unexpectedly, it is the affluent upper middle class, a group that earns more than $50,000 a year, that stands out as an exception to the rule among China's avid savers. A study by the McKinsey Consulting company found a surprising jump in the number of these relatively highly paid Chinese, who are suddenly interested in borrowing money. Thirty-one percent of this affluent class is now prepared to break with the cultural bias against borrowing, a bias that has traditionally regarded borrowing as a sign of weakness.[6] Only 19 percent of the people in this group would admit to wanting a loan only a few years ago, in 2004. The McKinsey findings showed a boom in the demand for loans as this select group sought bank loans for houses, investments, and education.

The growth of the middle class and the willingness of the upper middle class Chinese people to spend and borrow money is critically important for a host of economic and social reasons. A sizable middle class is universally believed to be an essential anchor for social and political stability in any emerging economy. A middle class that spends its income is especially important to China because the nation's economy needs to develop internal markets that are not vulnerable to fluctuations in demand for exported goods abroad.

Just as important is the development of a Chinese market for Western goods, a market that will address the growing chorus of complaints from the United States and Europe about the balance of payments problem. China's huge export surplus could spark a global economic crisis if the imbalance continues unabated. Avoiding such an international crisis is crucial for investors and working people of all developed economies.

Some economists also blame China's avid savers for sparking excessive economic growth and stimulating inflation. The boom on the Shanghai and Shenzhen stock markets is widely attributed to ordinary citizens seeking better returns on their money than the banks offer.

There are conflicting reports about the true size and growth rate of China's middle class. For example, McKinsey found that approximately 2 million Chinese belonged to the most affluent segment of the middle class. They also estimated that this wage-earning elite would grow at a rate of 15 percent a year.

But what about the most important bloc of Chinese consumers, those with the $10,000 to $12,000 incomes? The image of the frugal middle class may also be going the way of the bicycle. China appears to be embarking on a spending binge the likes of which the world has never seen. According to the National Bureau of Statistics, total retail sales exploded in 2007, growing at a rate of 15.9 percent from the year before.[7] For example, automobile sales are rising at a rate of 30 percent annually, while sales of home electronics and mobile phones are increasing at a rate of more than 20 percent annually. These are the kind of economic growth statistics that would make any Western nation green with envy. But many experts say that these figures understate the real rate of consumption in China because sales of services are not included, and services are one of the fastest-growing sectors of the economy.

Services are an essential element of any thriving middle class. Some service sectors provide financial and legal counsel, which tend to stabilize the economy and enhance wealth creation. Sales and marketing services facilitate the growth of new and innovative economic sectors. Personal services usually make life more enjoyable. A developed service sector is a hallmark of a stable, modern economy, and the fact that China is developing a service infrastructure bodes well for the future.

Consumerism Rising

The end of the bicycle kingdom will be obvious for the whole world to see by 2015. That's when China's consumer market is expected to become the second largest in the world. Only the United States, which now accounts for 42 percent of global consumption, will rank as a bigger consumer than China.[8] The Credit Suisse bank predicts that China's share of global consumption will rise to 14.1 percent of the total among the world's major economies by 2015, while America's share is projected to drop to 37.7 percent. It's not that U.S. consumers will lose their appetite for consumption. It's simply that the Chinese will begin to catch up and they will do so in huge numbers.

We have to envision China's immense potential for growth to fully understand these economic shifts in power and tectonic financial changes. Some sources estimate that only 110 million people out of a population of 1.3 billion are currently members of the consuming class.[9] Goldman Sachs predicts that this number, however, will grow exponentially to a staggering 650 million people by the year 2015. If Goldman Sachs is correct, the world will see a continuing explosion of economic activity in China, as retail consumption expands by almost 600 percent in less than a decade. The prospect is unprecedented, even by U.S. standards of consumerism.

Attaching some dollar figures to this exponential consumption curve yields awesome economic potential. China's true retail market is currently a relatively paltry $450 billion a year, or $346 per capita, which is about half that of Malaysia.[10] Assuming roughly 600 percent growth, a market for almost $3 trillion worth of retail goods could emerge in less than a decade. Such a development would have worldwide consequences, creating increased global demand for resources, finished products, and labor.

Make no mistake. The new China is emerging with buying power that would have thrilled China's capitalist pioneer, Deng Xiaoping. A revolution in spending and affluence is on its way. China's wealth explosion will indeed shake the world.

Riding the Wave of the Real Estate Boom

Another myth that goes hand in hand with China's old bicycle kingdom image is the perception that China's urban masses are content to live in cramped apartments or ancient neighborhoods called hutongs. In the oldest parts of most cities, China's hutongs form a maze of crowded alleyways and one-room homes clustered around communal courtyards.

These developments are currently being bulldozed on a vast scale to make way for high-rise buildings. They are being sacrificed as a part of China's capitalist revolution. Former premier Zhu Rongi conceived of the idea of using the housing market as a driver of economic growth.[11]

Ancient neighborhoods are disappearing especially quickly in Beijing, where image-conscious authorities have been eager to erase the traces of the old China in hopes of impressing Olympic visitors. Although some people will miss the tightly knit hutong neighborhoods, which were seen by tourists as a link to ancient China, no one will miss the poorly maintained, dingy apartment blocks that were once provided by the government or by state-owned enterprises.

Now an urban real estate boom has lifted many Chinese cities out of their dismal and dilapidated past.[12] City dwellers are finally permitted to own the property they inhabit and they are riding the wave of a real-estate buying frenzy. According to the *Wall Street Journal,* home ownership rates in Chinese cities are as high as 80 percent, exceeding U.S. home ownership rates of 69 percent. (Farmers are still not allowed to own the land they work on and must continue to lease it from the state, which assumed ownership of all land during the communist revolution.)

Real estate prices are rising rapidly, and construction projects are springing up to meet the demand. In every major city, a maze of construction cranes dominates the skyline as speculators rush to build new high-rises at a rate that often worries government officials, who are concerned about the development of a real estate bubble.

Although inflation does not appear to be a serious problem yet, except among foodstuffs, Chinese government economists appear to be as worried about the prospect of runaway inflation as former Federal Reserve chairman Alan Greenspan once was. Officials have repeatedly jacked up interest rates and bank reserve requirements in hopes of cooling off investment-driven growth in real estate and excess industrial capacity. Beijing has tried to clamp down on the issuance of new loans and building permits in hopes of cooling off the nation's property ownership craze, but with limited effect.

Chinese homeowners may not be rich by Western standards, but their incomes are rising two or three times faster than in other low-wage Asian countries.[13] Some companies are having trouble holding on to their most talented workers, and the situation could become worse. Westerners have always imagined that China has a virtually unlimited supply of low-cost labor. But the nation is rapidly moving from an era of labor surplus into an era of potential labor shortage.[14] The Chinese Academy of Social Sciences warns that the engine of the Chinese economic miracle—cheap labor—may be in short supply by 2010, triggering demands among workers for even higher wages and increasing competition for housing in prosperous urban areas.

If China does develop a labor shortage, there will plenty of even lower-wage countries waiting in line to take up the slack. Some jobs are already migrating to Vietnam, where factory wages average a meager $50 to $60 a month, which is half the level paid by factories along China's highly developed east coast.[15] But, as we will see, China is eager to move up the ladder of technically advanced economies with an eye to competing directly with the United States. The Chinese middle class has left the era of bicycles and hutongs in the past and most Chinese people who have not already joined the new elite are eager to move to the city, buy an apartment, and commute to work in a new car. China's ambitious dreams of national prosperity will continue to drive economic growth in every sector and company accessible to Western investors.

The Red Shadow

One of the persistent myths that has prevented many U.S. investors from feeling comfortable with investing in China is the looming shadow of communism, embodied in the outdated and somewhat frightening name, *Red China*. No system could be further from the principles of pure communism, yet the myth persists in many minds that the Chinese economic juggernaut is run by a communist clique similar to the old Maoist or Stalinist regimes.

Vocal critics of China have emerged in the U.S. media and the political arena, and they never miss an opportunity to invoke the specter of the Cold War by referring to China, formally known as the People's Republic of China, as Communist China or Red China.[16] The term is both misleading and increasingly irrelevant.

China is a communist country in name only. It is obviously true that the nation's central government is run by an elaborate centralized structure that still carries the name of the Communist Party of China. Much of the political apparatus that surrounds the president, Hu Jintao, is a leftover from the days of Chairman Mao. The president is still the General Secretary of the Communist Party, and he relies on the support of a pyramid of political party bodies, including the nine-member Politburo Standing Committee, which functions like the inner circle of the cabinet. Moving down the chain of command is the Central Committee and its powerful 24-member Politburo, a group that usually meets in secret sessions to work out policy. Finally, there is the National Congress of the Communist Party of China, whose 2,217 members meet every five years to discuss policy and approve leadership choices for the higher bodies. As impressive as this huge body may appear to be, the Congress has no real legislative power.

It would be fair to say that Western-style democracy is a long way off for the People's Republic of China. The closest thing to a democratic election is the selection of delegates to the National Congress by regional branches of the Communist Party. But choosing a delegate to attend a Congress that meets only twice a decade could hardly be called participatory democracy. Real leadership choices and national policy decisions are made by Politburo members and by high-ranking officials who head powerful bureaucracies with names like the National Development and Reform Commission (NDRC).

But the absence of democracy is not the same thing as communism. China could hardly be further from the basic principles of communism, an ideology that calls for the establishment of a society without social classes in which there is common ownership of the so-called means of production. China's new rich and the nation's middle class make up a privileged elite. Moving down the pecking order are factory workers and laborers. Near the bottom of the social hierarchy are migrant workers who often go hungry because they have chosen to seek employment in cities without the required papers or hokous. Sharing the bottom of the social ladder are the rural poor, who do not own the land they live upon. China claimed that it had eliminated poverty in 2000 because officials believed that almost no one earned an income of less than $77 a year or just 22 cents a day, an amount which Beijing deemed to be sufficient to enjoy the basic necessities of life.[17] But the World Bank defines absolute poverty as an income of less than a dollar a day and even Chinese authorities agreed that "26 million disabled people or those living in extremely bad natural environment areas" were indeed impoverished.

As is evident from the information presented here, the new China does not meet one test of real communism. The nation's extremes of wealth and poverty have created many distinct classes. Even one of China's official news outlets, the *Xinhua* news agency, acknowledges that the nation's rich are getting richer and the poor are getting poorer.[18] Just how far China has strayed from being a classless society was revealed recently in a survey by the Asia Development Bank.

Looking More and More Like the United States

The Asia Development Bank uses a mathematical measure of income inequality called the Gini coefficient, a standard also endorsed by the World Bank, to study social class rankings and economic equality. A low Gini coefficient indicates a society in which there is a considerable degree of equality. For example, a country with a Gini coefficient of zero would have achieved perfect income equality, in effect, a classless society. By contrast, a country with a Gini coefficient of one would indicate the opposite extreme in which a single person controls all wealth.

Obviously, no nation has ever achieved absolute equality, but it is revealing to discover where China stands on the spectrum. Chairman Mao would roll in his grave if he could see how far China has strayed from his proletarian vision. Inequality in China rose to an all-time high in the Asia Development Bank's latest report. China's Gini coefficient jumped to 0.473, up from 0.40 back in 1993. Compare that to the United States, the bastion of capitalist inequality, which had a Gini coefficient of 0.41 in the same survey. China now has greater income inequality than the United States.

China has indeed become an unequal, class-structured society. It has strayed very far from the communist ideal even though the government is clearly struggling to reduce the gap between rich and poor. The Asia Development Bank warns that the gap could slow the spread of prosperity, because the poorest people have less access to education, health care, bank loans, and other things needed to benefit from economic growth. The bank acknowledges that China's poorest people have benefited from the nation's economic boom but the incomes of the richest 20 percent of the population have grown much more quickly than those of the poor.

China's Capitalist Revolution

What about that other standard of real communism, that is, equal ownership of all things, especially the means of production? Most Chinese have enthusiastically embraced private ownership of everything from property to profitable companies. The stock markets in Shanghai and Shenzhen have become the subject of conversation at every level of society, from taxicabs to office towers. As *share fever* gripped Chinese cities during the internal stock market boom of

2006–2007, office managers complained publicly that no work was getting done while the markets were open because everyone was busy watching their shares rise and fall. Even gray-haired grandmothers, veterans of the Maoist years crammed into smoky brokerages, hoping to find the stocks that would make them rich.

Even in bookstores, I find no market for Chairman Mao's famous Little Red Book of slogans, except among tourists. Among the Chinese people crowding into bookshops, the overwhelming demand is for more business books, and Western authors are popular. From very technical volumes to the likes of *How to Win Friends and Influence People* by Dale Carnegie, young Chinese readers can't seem to get enough information.

Of course, many of the biggest businesses in China are at least partially state owned. That includes giant oil companies, banks, telephone systems, and manufacturers. Many of the companies whose shares trade on the New York Stock Exchange as American Depositary Receipts (ADRs) are majority-owned by the Chinese government. The very idea may smack of communism, but in practice, Chinese authorities have developed a taste for profitability, even in state-owned enterprises (SOEs), as they are called.

The current state of China's SOEs is a total turnaround from the situation a mere decade ago. During the early 1990s, Beijing looked on enviously as the so-called tiger economies of Asia raced ahead with their economic development and modernization. South Korea, Thailand, the Philippines, Malaysia, and even Indonesia followed in the footsteps of Japan, first building low-wage manufacturing economies and then progressing up the economic ladder. South Korea rose from a poor, war-ravaged agrarian society to a world-class auto-manufacturing nation in four decades. To the chagrin of the Chinese, even their renegade province, Taiwan, established itself as a world-leading source of advanced microchip design and manufacture.

While the world raced ahead, China's state-owned factories were chronic money losers. Some mega projects like the Three Gorges Dam were set into motion by huge injections of state capital. But profits and efficiency failed to materialize in China's lumbering SOEs. The solution was obvious among the Asian economic tigers and in China's own special economic zones, like Shenzhen. Building enterprises from the ground up and streamlining SOEs to earn profits by working efficiently was the only option.

Setting up more special economic zones within China turned out to be a boon to the growth of manufacturing and the creation of new companies. But special economic zones couldn't stop the hemorrhaging of money from the giant mills and factories left over from the days of Chairman Mao. What happened after 1997 is worth noting. In the space of just five years, Beijing laid off 25 million workers from the most heavily subsidized SOEs.[19] Many of the worst companies were shut down. The employment shocks that have hit the United States and Europe as a recent result of China's ascendancy don't begin to compare to the harsh economic discipline that China's leaders imposed on their own people. The government had realized that even state-run businesses needed to make a profit, preferably a healthy one.

The best evidence of the government's shifting mind-set is among the nation's biggest banks. Before China began the painful process of capitalist reforms, government-owned banks were treated like a policy arm of the leadership in Beijing. Money-losing enterprises were granted huge loans with no hope of ever seeing repayment. If the government wanted to prop up a corrupt and bloated factory, it would order a bank to write increasingly large loans. The banks themselves eventually seemed to be on the verge of collapse.

The scope of the problems in China's banking system was a state secret, but Standard & Poor's estimated that the total amount of nonperforming loans in the financial sector could have been as high as $864 billion in 2004.[20] Seeking to fill the black hole in the nation's banking industry, the government began bailing out the ailing financial giants. China Construction Bank (CCB) and Bank of China received $22.5 billion each. Industrial and Commercial Bank of China received a stunning $40 billion bailout. Bailouts of smaller banks are continuing to this day.

All the money in the world wouldn't have helped, of course, if the banks had continued to issue bad loans. Western bankers were very skeptical about the government's reforms. By 2006, Hong Kong investors were finally convinced of the success of the reform process when the once-failing banks were listed on the Hong Kong Stock Exchange. They generated some of the largest initial public offerings in history.

Capitalism is now flourishing and profits are pouring in among China's once-moribund state-owned enterprises. Giant companies like China Life (LFC), Aluminum Corporation of China (ACH), and Yanzhou Coal (YZC) have been among the top performers on U.S. stock exchanges, and I'm proud to say they have greatly enhanced the results of my own stock newsletter, the *China Stock Digest*. Their performance on U.S. markets is not based on a fad or a bubble like the dotcom fiasco. These are now real companies, earning huge profits.

During 2006, the nation's biggest SOEs booked record revenues and profits as they evolved from socialist control to capitalist management principles. The biggest and best of the SOEs, the so-called national champions, registered an increase in revenues of 20.1 percent during 2006. In total, they raked in a whopping $1.044 trillion. Profits rose almost as fast as revenues, up 18.2 percent for the year to $97 billion.[21]

Individual companies have delivered even greater profit increases. For example, during the first half of 2007, China Life (LFC) profits increased 160 percent from the same period the year before. Net profits for the first half of the year more than *doubled* to $3.1 billion. Guangshen Railway Company (GSH) says total revenues for the first half of 2007 increased 165.1 percent year over year to $611 million and profits increased 97.5 percent. Aluminum Corporation of China (ACH) reported an increase in revenues of 32 percent for the first half of 2007 as production soared. To any investor, these are breathtaking gains.

Investors in these SOEs have learned to live with the fact that the government is a controlling shareholder. Government participation is a factor that cuts both ways. Understanding that Beijing has embraced capitalism means that bureaucrats are eager to see profits. Successful managers are rewarded, and the central government benefits from dividends and share price increases. Officials will adjust state policy at times to assist the national champions, benefiting shareholders in the process.

There are 154 enterprises directly under the supervision of the Chinese central government through the State-owned Assets Supervision and Administration Commission (SASAC). If one were to include the assets of provincial governments, the number of SOEs increases to 424. The SASAC is primarily concerned with the profitability of its holdings. The central government generally shares this view, and it is working to reduce the total number of state-operated companies in hopes of streamlining the economy and increasing efficiency. Larger state enterprises benefit from this relationship, as competing firms are eliminated or the assets of smaller firms are folded into their portfolios.

But, at times, the SOE and government must balance the desire for profit and efficiency with the needs of the people. For example, China faces major air and water pollution problems. As a result, the government has stepped in to restrict bank loans for new capital investments in energy-intensive industries. Because of a policy written in 2007, top managers of the country's leading state-owned enterprises risk losing promotions or even their jobs if their companies fail to meet energy saving and pollution-reduction targets.[22]

Another example of the conflict between profit and meeting the needs of the people concerns commodity businesses. Prices of some commodities, such as gasoline, are capped by the central government to control inflation and prevent unrest in poorer parts of the country. As a result, the profits of refiners like Sinopec Shanghai Petrochemical (SHI) have been restrained.

In short, China's SOEs fall somewhat short of operating in an environment of total free market capitalism. At times, the government gives them a leg up over the competition. At other times, it places restrictions on corporations. Those restrictions are often no worse than Western antimonopoly laws or the increasingly strict environmental controls imposed by the U.S. government.[23] Of course, price controls have a much more socialistic flavor. The thing that matters to shareholders is profitability, and the Chinese government has put a premium on profit growth, sometimes at the expense of the environment.

Unleashing Private Investment

The government is also reducing its stake in national enterprises by selling shares on the open market. In early 2007, the government was expected to put $78 billion worth of shares up for sale on China's internal stock exchanges.[24] As the year progressed, nervousness over the size of the share sale faded when it became clear that share prices and corporate profits were rising inexorably. The total value of government holdings to be sold at market is estimated to be $250 billion, an amount called an overhang because of the potential for massive share sales to strain market liquidity and dilute share prices. So far, nothing of the kind has happened.

It remains most unlikely that the government will ever relinquish controlling interest in its national champion corporations.

Of course, not all Chinese businesses are run by SOEs. As the forces of capitalism have been gradually unleashed, thousands of private businesses have sprung up, and many of them have also returned spectacular profit growth and shareholder returns. Private companies have flourished in the Internet sector as entrepreneurs have rushed to create the Chinese equivalents of companies like Yahoo! (one Chinese version is called SINA), eBay (Alibaba is one Chinese equivalent), and Google (which is being beaten by Baidu). These Chinese brands serve a population of Internet users that will soon surpass that of the United States. Baidu is traded on the NASDAQ as BIDU and SINA is traded under its own initials, SINA.

Taiwan-based companies are also increasing their presence on the mainland. One of the world's biggest chipmakers, Taiwan Semiconductor (TSM), is building new factories in China to take advantage of the low cost of doing business there.

Changes in the law are even spurring the growth of one-man companies. Chinese media report that the growth of one-man firms has mushroomed since the introduction of the new *Company Law* in 2006. Before the law was passed, a self-employed person was exposed to unlimited liability if his business failed. The courts had the power to take all of the business owner's possessions, including those of his family, to make good on losses and debts. Under the popular new law, the liability of one-man corporations is limited to the amount of registered capital, an amount set by law at approximately $13,000.

While capitalism flourishes at all levels, from giant state enterprises to one-man companies, the Chinese people face challenges caused by the collapse of social systems that existed under the communist system. Providing health care, education, and old-age pensions used to be the responsibility of employers, and under Chairman Mao all employers belonged to the state. When succeeding administrations dismantled the communist system, they shifted much of the responsibility for these social services to individuals and families. Even for young families, health care currently ranks among the most important expenditures in the household budget. In 2004, private spending accounted for 64 percent of health-care expenditures in China.[25] Many older Chinese simply decide to avoid treatment because they cannot afford it.

The Future Capital of Capitalism

China has veered further from the dictates of communism and socialism than many western European nations. The government has said it is committed to make sure that everyone has access to good health care, and it has even called in U.S. management consultants to help it construct a workable system. New initiatives are being implemented to help the rural poor educate their children. A viable social safety net will ultimately be essential as China's population ages. Because of the one-child policy, it is estimated that the ratio of workers to retirees will decline from six to one in 2000 to just two to one in 2040.[26] Ironically, China has strayed so far from its old cradle-to-grave socialist policies that the government has realized that the pendulum must swing back. More funding is being directed toward social programs as Beijing realizes that a greater level of financial security is essential to maintain stability in society.

Without question, the bicycle kingdom is long gone. China today is an exciting hybrid of new capitalism, ancient tradition, and a smattering of reminders from the stultifying years of communism. It's true that dyed-in-the-wool Marxists still remain in a few positions of influence, calling for China to turn back the clock. But that will never happen.

In some ways, China's central government is as tough as Chairman Mao's so-called dictatorship of the people. Critics of the government, from Internet bloggers to accredited journalists, are routinely silenced and sometimes imprisoned. It is a rigidly authoritarian regime and it is not democratic in any way that we would recognize. But that does not make it a communist power in any meaningful sense, except in name.

Beijing has decided that economic development, social stability, and the survival of the regime are critically important principles. Leading academics and China watchers believe that the nation's educated and prosperous middle class wants no part of open democracy for the time being because the peasant populace of the countryside is uneducated and unprepared.[27] The elite fear that the masses would be too easily swayed by demagogues and corruption. They look at the collapse of another communist superpower, the Soviet Union, and feel relieved that political revolution took a backseat to capitalist economic reforms.

It's true that the portrait of Chairman Mao still looms over China's Tian'anmen Square. But the Great Helmsman's influence has changed over the years. His slogans have disappeared from the public consciousness. China's old and failed economy has been wrenched away from the Marxist principles of communism to make the new China the capitalist wonder of the world.

CHAPTER

4

The Coming Financial Flood

The want of money is the root of all evil.
—Samuel Butler

The economic events that are moving China forward are also serving to push America off center stage. We have already seen the decline of the United States' middle class caused by the exportation of entire manufacturing sectors because China is producing many products and goods that are taking away the jobs of many average U.S. workers.

Don't believe me? Here is a list of industries that used to be based in the United States that are now long gone or disappearing, leaving behind empty and crumbling factory buildings.[1]

- Adhesives and sealants
- Auto parts, including electrical assemblies
- Baby goods
- Bedding
- Bicycles and motorcycles
- Building materials and hardware
- Clothing
- Computer parts and computer monitors
- Construction equipment, including pumps, drills, and chainsaws
- Crafts and small gifts

- Cameras
- Electronics, including televisions, and radios
- Eyeglass frames and sunglasses
- Fashion accessories
- Fitness and bodybuilding equipment
- Food products
- Furniture and fiberboard
- Home healthcare products
- Household goods and tools
- Industrial tools
- Jewelry
- Kitchen appliances and parts
- Laboratory equipment
- Lamps and bulbs
- Machines, including generators and air conditioners
- Office supplies, equipment, and machinery
- Outdoor home tools and entertainment items
- Paper goods
- Pigments and specialty chemicals
- Police and military equipment
- Shipbuilding
- Shoes and leather goods
- Small motors and other mechanical devices
- Telephones
- Textiles and fibers
- Tires and rubber goods
- Toys and recreational goods

How We Helped Create the Flood

The *Made in China* label is everywhere, in every field of endeavor, whether you are aware of it or not and Americans helped put it there. As you can see in Figure 4.1, the surge of Chinese imports has become a tidal wave in the field of consumer goods within the past 15 years. In today's economy, China accounts for 80 percent of the United States' toy market, 50 percent of the footwear market, almost 50 percent of the consumer electronics market, and 12 percent of the clothing market, making it the number one source for clothing sold in the United States.[2] Sales of Chinese-made DVD players, mobile phones, and personal computers to American

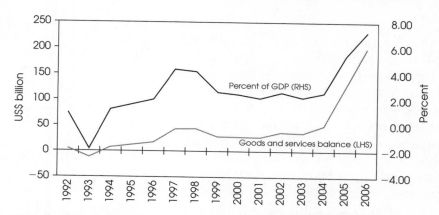

Figure 4.1   Net Exports of Goods and Services, 1992–2006
Source: National Bureau of Statistics of China, China Statistical Yearbook 2006; International
Monetary Fund; International Financial Statistics; CEIC.

consumers are soaring. According to Nicholas Lardy of the Institute
for International Economics, U.S. imports of notebook computers
from China increased exponentially from $5 million to more than
$7 billion between 1998 and 2004. During the same period, sales of
Chinese-made mobile phones rose from $75 million to more than
$4 billion; DVD player imports from China rose from less than half
a million dollars to $3 billion; and sales of made-in-China digital
cameras jumped from $7 million to $3 billion.[3]

It wasn't supposed to happen this way. For centuries, Western
businessmen have regarded China as a vast potential market and
a source of profits, not competition. In the 1800s, a British writer
famously remarked, "If only we could persuade every person in
China to lengthen his shirt-tail by a foot, we could keep the mills of
Lancashire working around the clock."[4] Sadly, the mills of Lancashire
are a distant memory and the remaining textile mills of North and
South Carolina are also disappearing as China becomes "the major
textile exporter to the world."[5]

With relatively few exceptions, early Western efforts to turn
China into the world's largest consumer paradise have been met
with opposition, even though the dream lives on in books like *One
Billion Customers* by James McGregor, formerly of the *Wall Street
Journal.* The reality is that China prefers to sell goods to the world,
not to buy finished goods from other countries. China wants the
employment and the revenue that comes from producing consumer

products for six billion potential customers in every corner of the globe. To this day, Chinese corporations are reaping the fruits of this strategy with exceptional profit growth, as shown in Figure 4.2.

Many early attempts to penetrate the Chinese consumer market ended in fiasco because Chinese authorities insisted that manufacturers who wanted access to Chinese markets form joint ventures with moribund state-owned enterprises. For example, the 1980s attempt by American Motors to become the first U.S. automaker with access to the Chinese market was a dismal and unprofitable experience for all concerned.[6] During the 1990s, Western businessmen recounted a litany of frustrations as they tried to build enterprises around the endlessly tempting lure of one billion Chinese customers. Instead of hungry markets and eager partners, they found that "signed agreements and memoranda of understanding turned out to be worthless; court rulings were not enforced; state-owned enterprises were exempt from costly environmental regulations; expensive licenses, processed by lackadaisical bureaucrats, were required at every turn; counterfeiting and abuse of intellectual property rights were rampant."[7]

But China proved to be a much easier nut to crack for the thousands of foreign companies that decided to set up factories on the Chinese mainland to manufacture or assemble products and ship them out to the world. The bureaucrats of Beijing were willing to roll out the red carpet for foreigners who provided jobs and technology without demanding access to domestic markets. According to

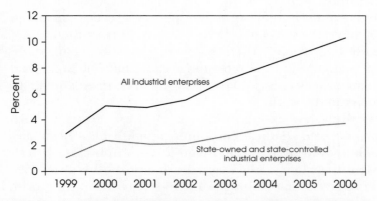

Figure 4.2   Industry Profits as Percent of GDP 1999–2006
Source: National Bureau of Statistics of China, China Statistical Yearbook 2006; CEIC.

a respected French think tank, half of all Chinese exports resulted from the processing and assembly of imported parts by 2007.[8]

It's not just parts and raw materials that foreign businesses are sending to China. Entire factories—which are the means of production—are being disassembled, crated, and shipped from the United States and Europe to be rebuilt thousands of miles away as modern components of the Chinese industrial engine. Along with the machines and their components, the West is sending away the blueprints and the technological expertise that went into the design and operation of the modern economy's industrial muscle and sinew.[9] The Chinese government, increasingly dominated by technocrats, fully understands the importance of acquiring Western technology so they can penetrate Western markets with desirable goods. Newly learned Western technologies are being put to use to serve the Chinese—the very same consumers that Western entrepreneurs have coveted for more than a century. It goes without saying that Westerners export jobs along with the machinery and technical expertise underpinning America's and Europe's industrial base.

Chinese buyers are also snapping up entire companies. Wanxiang Group owns an auto parts maker in Rockford, Illinois, and the Chinese computer maker Lenovo purchased IBM's entire laptop business in 2004 for a surprisingly modest $1.25 billion. Lenovo became the third-largest personal computer maker in the world as it grew to build machines for IBM's existing markets as well as the vast Chinese and Asian markets. Lenovo computers started making a strong appearance in North America during the 2007 Christmas season.

Western resources are also attractive to cash-rich Chinese buyers. In 2005, the China National Offshore Oil Company (CNOOC) tried to buy Unocal. An uproar in Congress and in the media about foreign ownership of U.S. resources forced CNOOC to withdraw its $18.5 billion bid. A substantially lower bid by Chevron actually won the day. But smaller resource deals have garnered much less bad publicity. A deal between the Cleveland-Cliffs Company and Laiwu Steel saved 500 U.S. jobs at a bankrupt mine in Minnesota's Iron Ridge.[10] The deal cost the Chinese partners the equivalent of $43 million and provided a supply of ore essential for China's booming steel industry. We can expect this resource buying trend to spread throughout the United States and Europe as China flexes its growing economic muscle.

The Next "Asian Tiger"

The United States is not the only country being affected by China's surge to economic power. China now rivals both Japan and South Korea in one of Asia's core industries, shipbuilding. During the first half of 2007, China's shipbuilding industry posted a 151 percent increase in profits, raking in a remarkable $848 million over six months. China is recognized as the world's number three shipbuilder, but growing demand for oceangoing transport has boosted the industry to unprecedented heights. Measured by new and existing orders, China's shipbuilding industry has vaulted ahead of Japan and South Korea to become number one in the world.

The remarkable rise of the post–World War II Japanese economy is one of the models that Chinese leaders, economists, and businessmen are hoping to emulate on a much larger scale. China looked on with jealousy as the so-called Asian tiger economies of Japan, South Korea, Taiwan, Singapore, and Hong Kong led the Asia-Pacific region out of postwar economic stagnation. The new economies of Malaysia, Indonesia, Thailand, and the Philippines followed suit while China struggled to shake off the remnants of the communist economic system.

The turning point for China was likely the East Asian financial crisis that ripped through the economies of the tiger nations during 1997 and 1998. Sparked by a collapse of the Thai currency, the baht, the financial crisis dragged down the currencies and stock markets of many Southeast Asian nations. The crisis put an end to the explosive growth phase called the Asian economic miracle, and it provided an opening for China's economic rise. China's currency did not collapse because the nation's currency, the yuan, was pegged to the dollar, and the Chinese central bank had sufficient liquidity to maintain the peg and defend itself against currency speculators.

Having survived the economic tsunami that has left some of the Asian tigers still struggling, China's leadership realized the next step had to be a decisive move up the value chain. Assembling computers and cell phones is not the same thing as designing them, manufacturing sophisticated components, or marketing the end product in wealthy Western nations. Chinese businessmen and leaders realized that that's where the money is. As such, they eagerly began creating, making, and producing lavish goods that were in demand from foreign markets. They manufactured these goods with low production costs and then exported them to Western countries at a competitive price, which often resulted in a lucrative profit.

The "China Price"

China has gained access to Western markets, but the downside has been relentless pressure to reduce production costs every single year. The phrase *China price* sprang up in the context of the endless search for lower prices, first by pitting American workers against Chinese laborers and then by pitting dollar-a-day Chinese workers and their employers against each other in a competitive race to the bottom.

There's nothing wrong with price competition in a market economy as long as quality standards are maintained at every level of the production and marketing process. Certainly, unskilled workers in poor countries are generally grateful for employment that provides a living wage. But it's easy to see why Chinese leaders are eager to see the nation's economy move up the value chain.

The furor over the recall of Chinese-made toys contaminated with lead paint during 2007 brought home the perils of being a low-cost manufacturer. Chinese manufacturers all along the production chain took virtually all of the blame and suffered most of the harsh economic consequences for the lead contamination. American media paid little attention to Chinese assemblers' complaints about being forced to continually shave production costs and produce goods using flawed Western designs while the Western companies at the top of the pyramid reaped huge profits and assumed minimal responsibility for product testing. An executive from one of the companies at the center of the substandard Chinese goods controversy, Mattel, was forced to make a humiliating apology on Chinese television, admitting that most of the problems with his company's products had been caused by Mattel's own design flaws, not by substandard Chinese manufacturing processes.

Of course, nothing excuses the decision to use lead as an ingredient in a child's toy. But it's worth looking at problems from more than one perspective. To use a more benign example, it is quite true that giant big box stores like Wal-Mart have been indispensable to the emerging Chinese economy. In little more than a decade, countless factories and armies of unskilled Chinese workers have been able to produce and sell products within competitive Western economies through companies like Wal-Mart without establishing their own supply chains, product development departments, branding campaigns, or marketing strategies. Doing so within China would have taken decades, meaning retailers like Wal-Mart have been an integral part of the Chinese economic miracle.

By the same token, low-cost production in China has been essential to the American retailer's rise to global dominance. Cheap goods from Wal-Mart have also benefited penny-pinching U.S. consumers. Chinese-made goods have become so predominant in Wal-Mart, a chain that used to pride itself on selling American-made goods, the company might as well call itself China-Mart. American consumers have benefited from lower prices, and it has been argued, not without justification, that many products now made in China will never again be produced in the United States because there are many other low-wage countries that would happily take the place of Chinese manufacturers if they could. U.S. workers simply could not compete.

Who Pays the *Real* China Price?

China's pollution crisis provides yet another compelling incentive for Beijing to push its capitalist class to move up the value chain. The scale of the nation's environmental problems is so great that it almost defies description. The World Health Organization (WHO) calls China's air pollution the deadliest in the world. WHO blames China's air pollution for killing an appalling number of people, 656,000 every year, with almost 100,000 more dying from the effects of water pollution.[11] In a ranking of the 20 most polluted cities in the world, the World Bank claims that 16 of those cities are in China. Ninety percent of China's urban groundwater is contaminated, and 75 percent of the surface water flowing through Chinese cities is too polluted to be used for either drinking or fishing.[12] By the government's own admission, 100 of China's 660 cities face extreme water shortages because of the pollution crisis.[13] Half of the nation's population, almost 700 million people in 278 cities, live without any form of sewage treatment.[14] China is also the world's largest emitter of sulfur dioxide, the main component of acid rain. China is even surpassing the United States as the world's biggest emitter of greenhouse gasses.

China's economy has already begun to suffer as a result of the pollution crisis. In an effort to measure the economic damage caused by pollution, the State Environmental Protection Administration (SEPA) began calculating something called the Green GDP, which measures China's extraordinary annual growth in its gross domestic product and subtracts the real economic cost of pollution. The country's first green GDP report in 2004 showed losses of $54 billion caused by pollution, which accounts for more than 3 percent of the year's total GDP. Based on this calculation, China's economic growth doesn't look so good. Annual double-digit increases were suddenly called into question. We can only assume that the problem has become much worse. In March of 2007, senior Beijing officials ordered the environmental agency to keep the latest green GDP figures a secret.[15] Many provinces and cities involved in compiling the report said they wanted to pull out of the green initiative because they were afraid that regional economic growth could be affected.

The pollution crisis is contributing to a broader shift in the direction of China's economic growth. According to SEPA, a crackdown on polluters resulted in more than 3,000 companies being shut down in 2006 and more than 8,000 being punished in 2007. Hundreds of projects that would have damaged the environment, including new steel mills and power plants, have been canceled. State-owned enterprises have been ordered to cut pollution discharges by 10 percent and energy consumption by 10 percent no later than 2010.[16]

In a new industrial initiative, financial institutions are being encouraged to provide loans to new environmental protection and pollution reduction projects. New restrictions are being imposed on exports that require large amounts of energy or generate large amounts of pollution, such as steel, nonferrous metals, cement, and petrochemicals. China is also set to make large investments in pollution control technology. Such policy shifts are slow in coming but they will guide our investment choices. One of our best investment performers has been Suntech Power (STP), a company that makes pollution-free solar electricity panels.

China's leaders have resorted to blaming the West for global pollution problems, and their argument is not entirely without merit. Looking at the situation through China's eyes, Western nations have been busy polluting the planet's air and water for more than a century. While Europe and the United States rose as industrial powers, burning spectacular amounts of coal and oil in the process, China was largely an agrarian nation, stuck in the Middle Ages, due in large part to the previously mentioned 100 years of humiliation. Now, as the Chinese see it, their moment has come to match the West by rising to industrial and political greatness. The onus is on the West to clean up its act first, at least from Beijing's point of view.

But China faces environmental challenges too great to ignore. The global problem of climate change can be attributed partly to Western pollutants discharged over the past century, but blaming the West doesn't solve the problem. Just as in the United States' early years of industrialization, severe internal pollution has been regarded as the price of progress in modern China. The pioneering capitalists and captains of U.S. and British industry cared little about polluting the air and water when there was a profit to be made. Now China faces the problem of balancing economic growth against environmental concerns in an accelerated time frame. During a period of exploding energy demand and a growing pollution crisis, I predict a great future for Chinese companies like Suntech Power (STP) in renewable energy fields.

Much like a massive ship moving at high speed, the Chinese economy will need time to change course. The obvious long-term goal is to shift the economy to a less polluting, value-added foundation. For the time being, the nation's ravenous energy needs will demand the construction of more coal-fired electricity-generating plants. General Electric (GE) has carved out a multibillion-dollar market for gas-powered turbines in China, turbines that will generate much cleaner energy than coal.

In a typical Chinese business strategy, Beijing has found a way to leverage its turbine purchases to develop new high-technology industries. In 2003, GE won the bidding under a technology transfer arrangement to become China's leading supplier of sophisticated gas turbines.[17] In a joint venture agreement with the Harbin Power Equipment Company and the Shenyang Liming Aero-Engine Group, GE will engage their Chinese partners in the construction and assembly of its most advanced gas turbines. China will acquire considerable technological expertise from its U.S. partner, although GE says it retains the most important industrial secrets of building high-energy turbines.

Speaking at the World Economic Forum in 2007, Premier Wen Jiabao admitted to an audience of thousands of global business leaders that China faced problems of excessively rapid economic growth, depletion of resources, environmental degradation, and mounting pressure on prices. "To resolve these problems," he said, "we are putting into practice scientific thinking on development and an innovation-based model of development."[18] In other words, China is determined to move up the value chain and into economic territory dominated by the United States and other Western nations.

Climbing the Economic Value Chain

China's preference for high-tech industries continues to increase as the nation's environmental and economic challenges grow more difficult. The 352,000 engineering graduates that pour out of China's universities every year are the heart and soul of China's high tech future. Their numbers dwarf the United States's graduation rates of 137,000 engineers per year.[19] Engineers make up the bulk of Beijing's technocratic administration, and they are creating the framework of China's economic future.

In its effort to encourage high-technology companies to establish a base in China, the government has offered a variety of tax breaks and incentives as well as access to the domestic market. The Chinese Ministry of Commerce estimates that more than $70 billion worth of foreign investments have been pumped into the nation's high-tech sector, generating a total of $192 billion worth of exports.[20] Evidence of the growing importance of high technology to China's industrial model is the volume of exports from the sector. Beijing says more than 43 percent of all exports by foreign-funded businesses were from the high-tech sector, an increase of 18.2 percent in just five years.

Foreign firms are doing much more than helping to establish China's rising position in the manufacturing chain. They are helping to fund the research and development (R&D) that underpins any high technology enterprise. Multinational companies have set up no fewer than 750 R&D centers in China.[21] Some estimates say the number of foreign research and development offices is nearing 1,000.

The names of the companies that are sending a part of their research and development budgets to Shanghai, Shenzhen, and

Beijing are among the best-known brands in the world. They include Oracle, Nokia, Panasonic, Nortel, and Hewlett-Packard. One of the largest investments is from Microsoft, which plans to invest $100 million in China for its own operations in addition to the $65 million the company has already invested in Chinese-based software enterprises. Microsoft China is expected to increase its Chinese workforce from 1,000 to 3,000 by 2012.[22]

Another core of most advanced Western economies, the pharmaceutical and biotechnology industries, are also helping fund the research and development movement in China. Novartis and Agilent have established R&D centers. Eli Lilly has struck a drug development deal with Chi-Med of Shanghai. Chi-Med is also working with Merck and Procter & Gamble. Staging clinical trials of new drugs in China has become an increasingly popular trend for multinational drug developers because of the relative ease of finding participants in China's vast population and because of the much lower cost of conducting trials there.[23]

One of the biggest breakthroughs in China's effort to go high tech is the construction of a $2.5 billion Intel (INTC) chipset plant in Dalian. The factory, dubbed FAB-68, will be one of the largest single foreign investments ever made in China. Intel says it is making the investment in FAB-68 because China is its second-largest market after the United States and is expected to be the world's biggest information technology market by 2010.[24] Like Taiwanese chip manufacturers, Intel will not use its most advanced technologies in its Chinese branch plant because of concerns over the rampant theft of intellectual property in China.

China also has its eye on another high-tech industry of the U.S. economy, the aircraft industry. Boeing says China is now the company's largest foreign supplier of parts. More than 3,000 people are working for Boeing in joint ventures, supplying products under $2.5 billion worth of contracts.[25] Boeing and Airbus have little choice but to enter into joint ventures with Chinese partners if they want to sell aircraft in that country. Boeing estimates that China will need more than 2,900 new airplanes to meet the growing demand from Chinese airlines, so the incentive to transfer some technology is very considerable.

Not surprisingly, China is diving into the fastest-growing segment of the aircraft industry with an airplane design of its own. The new ARJ21 is a small, regional jet that will compete with successful aircraft in the same category produced by Bombardier of Canada and Embraer of Brazil. The first ARJ21, a 90-seat jet, is expected to roll off the assembly lines of a company that still bears the old communist-era name China Aircraft Corporation 1. In 2009, Chinese carriers will begin flying the aircraft with engines made by General Electric and foreign-made avionics. It will shock no one to learn that China increased the tax on imports of small commercial jets several years ago, forcing both Bombardier and Embraer to strike joint venture agreements for the assembly and production of regional jets with China Aviation Industry Corporation 1.[26]

Imitation Is Not Always Flattery—It's Stealing

President Hu Jintao proclaimed in 2006 that "independent innovation is the core of national competitiveness," but *foreign* innovation is still the true engine of China's effort to become a world-class technology leader. While it is true that China's investment in research and development is projected to rise from 1.34 percent of GDP to 2.5 percent by 2020, the nation still isn't getting a lot of innovation from its homegrown efforts. According to the State Intellectual Property Office (SIPO), only 0.03 percent of Chinese enterprises actually own the key technologies for which they claim to have intellectual property rights. Despite China's enormous foreign trade volume, only 2 percent of that trade is in patented Chinese high-technology products.

From a global perspective, China has finally made it into the top 10 lists of nations applying for patents. The World Intellectual Property Office (WIPO) says China's patent applications increased by 44 percent in 2005, putting the Chinese ahead of Canada, Australia, and Italy in innovation. But the United States is still the world leader with a total of 45,000 applications for inventions and creations, a huge lead over China's 2,452 applications.

Foreign innovators also lead in the number of patent applications filed within China. SIPO says Chinese innovators produced only 18 percent of internal patent applications for inventions compared to 86 percent from foreign companies.[27] An astonishing 99 percent of Chinese enterprises have never applied for a patent, and 60 percent do not own their own trademarks, according to the State Intellectual Property Office. China's rapid industrial modernization has not yet been accompanied by expertise in branding and marketing.

One of the sad ironies of patenting an invention in China is that the patent office is often a first stop for intellectual property thieves. In fact, patents sometimes serve as a production guide for intellectual property pirates. Companies that file for patents in Beijing risk losing their technology to copycats before they can manage to bring their products to market in China. Despite almost monthly pledges by state officials to protect intellectual property (IP), counterfeiting of foreign technology, trademarked goods, films, and music brazenly continues.

The problem of protecting intellectual property is especially severe in the auto industry. Blatant piracy first surfaced at a Chinese auto show in 2003 when an obvious copy of the General Motors *Spark* (known in the United States as the *Aveo*) appeared under the Chinese brand name *QQ*. To the astonishment of GM executives, the *QQ* was such a perfect copy of the *Spark* that the doors could be exchanged and fit perfectly. The tiny *QQ* sells for approximately $5,000, about half the cost of the *Spark*. General Motors and Chery, the Chinese manufacturer of the *QQ*, quietly reached a settlement after the U.S. automaker accused the Chinese company of brazenly copying its *Spark* model.[28] Although critics accuse the Chinese version of miserably failing crash tests, it has now become one of the most common sights on the roads of Chinese cities. Other joint venture car companies, including BMW and Chrysler, have also accused their partners of stealing the designs of their luxury models and producing copies.[29]

Dan Koeppel of *Popular Science* investigated the industrial bootlegging business in China and found that some factories, which were legitimately producing products for Western contractors with their day shift, would simply hire a second shift for the sole purpose of counterfeiting. This *ghost shift* would secretly use the plant's entire facilities to make near-perfect copies of the brand name products that were churned out legally during the day. In other cases, large teams of engineers would be assigned to pick apart and duplicate the workings of high-tech exports, beating the foreign contractor to market with his own technology. Koeppel's report, titled "China's iClone," includes a disturbing video of a brand new Chinese copy of Apple's leading-edge product, the iPhone. The clone was available in China shortly after Apple brought its product to market with a global publicity blitz. The sad fact is this: China may not be beating the West in innovation, but it is snapping up the crown jewels of America's industrial base and innovative genius by hook and by crook.

China is educating armies of new engineers to act as the nation's foot soldiers in the long march to supremacy in high technology. But without a culture that encourages innovation and a legal system that vigorously protects intellectual property, China's innovators will lag behind the competition in leading-edge industries. There is very little incentive for Chinese entrepreneurs to design, test, and market new products when it is so much cheaper to produce imitations.

Prosecutions for dealing in stolen intellectual property rarely amount to more than a slap on the wrist. In effect, Beijing is tacitly giving counterfeiters the go-ahead because somewhere between 10 and 30 percent of the nation's GDP is believed to come from piracy and counterfeiting. Domestically, piracy accounts for as much as 20 percent of retail sales.[30] The International Intellectual Property Alliance estimates piracy rates remain at more than 90 percent across all copyright industries.

China cannot have it both ways. At the World Economic Forum in Dailan, Premier Wen Jiabao appealed to foreign companies to bring more research and development to his nation. He pledged to protect their rights, "particularly intellectual property rights." But Western businessmen know that the system is often rigged against them. Even with the best of intentions from the top levels of government, the courts and provincial governments (local authorities and the police) are extremely reluctant to impose a real crackdown. That means top-tier companies like Intel (INTC) and Taiwan Semiconductor Manufacturing (TSM) will be extremely reluctant to produce cutting-edge products on the Chinese mainland. The plants they are building now will be relegated to churning out chips that are two or three generations behind the leading edge.

Your Blueprint for an Ark

There is no question that the world's economic center of gravity is shifting toward China. Sixty-three percent of the huge increase in China's foreign exports over the past decade comes from foreign companies and joint ventures doing business in China. Among them are branch operations of 51,000 American companies.[31] Despite the many problems that face China and face companies doing business in China, we are witnessing the dawn of the Chinese century. It makes sense to invest accordingly. Smart investors are diversifying their holdings into select Chinese stocks and taking a long second look at their holdings in U.S. firms.

China's most profitable enterprises are not those that process goods for foreign contractors. They typically operate on razor-thin margins. The big money is still among the modernized enterprises that were once entirely state-owned. The best of these companies enjoy revenues in the billions of dollars. They may have relinquished their monopolies, but the best of China's national champion corporations still have dominant shares of the energy, telecommunications, and resources sectors. Some have risen to join the ranks of the largest companies in the world, and many of them are easily available to investors on the New York Stock Exchange as ADRs.

There are also fast-growing private companies emerging in the newest sectors of the Chinese economy. There is fierce competition among companies staking out their territory in Internet commerce, advertising, security, gaming, brewing, and computer manufacturing. Generally speaking, companies that have no state ownership are listed as ADRs on the NASDAQ exchange. They may be rising rapidly, but they tend to be the more volatile Chinese issues.

As we conclude our broad overview of the unprecedented hybrid that is the new Chinese economy, we're going to take a closer look at the sectors that may be appropriate for diversified investments. Becoming your own China stock guru requires a substantial amount of background information, but fortunately, it has been my pleasure to do the legwork for you. Read on to find out more about where the money is being made in the new China.

CHAPTER

Becoming a Guru

Money is a headache, and money is the cure.
—Everett Mamor

After reading the first four chapters of this book, any thinking person would agree that China will eventually become the world's largest economy. The evidence is as clear as it is overwhelming. Armed with this insight, however, we need ask ourselves a fundamental question:

Will we allow China's unstoppable rise in economic power to increase or decrease our wealth? More simply put, will we be China winners or China losers?

This is a question we need ask both as a nation, and as individuals. Just look around the country where you live. The impact of China's rise on American families is already everywhere to be seen. You need travel no farther than Detroit, Michigan, to meet countless *China losers* among the ranks of unemployed auto industry workers. The old-style U.S. $65-an-hour manufacturing salaries cannot possibly compete with Chinese factory workers who typically work just as hard as we do but who instead make that $65 wage, not per hour, but for an entire month of labor. In the southern United States, textile mills and shoe factories that existed for generations now stand idle. These unfortunate people are sometimes referred to as *China losers*—that is, the victims of a new breed of hard-working

Chinese capitalists, each of whom is determined to earn their own piece of the American dream.

Yet being a *China loser* need not be the future for our nation in general, nor for you, the reader, in particular. All too frequently, I marvel at a blunder or newly missed opportunity that we, as a nation, make in our national policies toward China. Think about it. A nation of 1.3 billion people is desperately yearning for our style of economic freedom and for our help in implementing the capitalist system that created the American dream. They are willing to make almost anyone smart enough to recognize the opportunity from this tectonic shift in world affairs fabulously wealthy.

Clearly most Americans just don't get it when it comes to China. Becoming a *China winner* (or dare we say . . . a China guru) may make you extremely rich, but it may make you unpopular.

> **Guru** – *noun* **2 a :** a teacher and especially intellectual guide in matters of fundamental concern **b :** one who is an acknowledged leader or chief proponent **c :** a person with knowledge or expertise.—Merriam-Webster

This is because almost everywhere we turn, we see self-serving politicians and self-proclaimed *nationalists* on cable TV demonizing those yearning Chinese masses who strive to be just like us. The real tragedy is that for every *China loser* I see, there could have been a *China winner* in his place . . . a *China winner* who understands what is going on in the world around him and finds a way to profit from it.

To illustrate how one can be a *China winner,* consider the example of Hong Kong. During the 1980s, as China opened its doors to foreign capitalists, one of the first groups to benefit were the successful industrialists of Hong Kong. At that time, Hong Kong had many factories churning out consumer products that were exported worldwide. They quickly realized, though, that the salaries paid in Hong Kong could not possibly compete with the ridiculously low labor rates paid on the Chinese mainland. What did the Hong Kong industrialists do? They moved their factories into China and brought the profits home to benefit the Hong Kong economy. Today, almost 30 years later, you do not see an endless stream of unemployed factory workers collecting unemployment benefits and living on the streets of Hong Kong. You see, instead, a prosperous city, with a robust service economy, very high per capita high wages, and an unemployment rate of less than 5 percent. In other words, Hong Kong residents adapted to focus on their strengths and became *China winners,* not *China losers.* Those of us in the United States would be wise to follow their example.

For now, though, we will leave foreign policy questions to the diplomats. Our focus at the moment is making sure that you, dear reader, become one of the China winners. Together, we will protect our families and increase our fortunes. Together, we shall profit handsomely from China's unstoppable rise on the world economic stage. No *China loser* status for us, thank you very much!

What If Bill Gates Had Been Born in China?

It's amazing when you stop to consider how much the world has changed over the past 25 years. As a result of the fall of totalitarian state-run economies, living standards throughout the world have been raised. In fact, it's no coincidence that the two areas of the world with the most poverty—the Middle East and Africa—are the last to undergo a capitalist revolution. It's also no coincidence that these noncapitalist areas are hotbeds for extremism and violence, because capitalism is the path to peace and prosperity, and as more nations have embraced the free market, the world has become a more egalitarian place.

Bill Gates is no beauty contest winner, but nevertheless, he makes a good poster boy for capitalism. After all, he used his *mind* to build the world's largest fortune—in excess of $40 billion— and his company, Microsoft, made hundreds of millionaires and increased the world's productivity in the process. Gates is now giving away his billions to global charities, and his efforts will undoubtedly improve countless lives throughout the world. Bill Gates exemplifies the fact that economics is not a zero sum game and that a rising tide can lift all boats. His story demonstrates the win-win-win proposition of capitalism. But just think: What if Gates had been born in China instead of the United States?

Gates himself coined a term for this inequality of circumstance— the *ovarian lottery.* Gates means by this that in the past, it would have been better to be born an average Joe in the United States than a genius almost anywhere else in the world. Just think if Gates had been born in the Soviet Union under Stalin. In all likelihood, he would have never earned $40,000, let alone $40 billion. But more than Gates himself, it is the world that would have lost out.

Before the fall of the Berlin Wall, half of the world was under totalitarian rule. This means that there was probably an Eastern hemisphere Gates to equal the West's version, but instead of making hundreds of billions for himself and others, the East's Gates toiled away in obscurity since birth; his talent and ambition crushed under the heel of a left-wing regime. But since capitalism has swept through most of the world—including China—Gates himself has said, "Now, I would rather be a genius born in China than an average guy born in Poughkeepsie."

Think about it: The next generation will have more than twice the number of people from which a Bill Gates or Warren Buffett may emerge. Imagine the compounding effect of a Chinese Gates and a Chinese Buffett to match their Western counterparts. The world's wealth will not just double, it will multiply exponentially, and everyone in the world will be better off for it. But who will make the *most* money? Will it be those who invest in the next Microsoft and get in early?

The split-adjusted value of a share of Microsoft in 1986 was just $0.08. If you had invested a mere $3,000 in MSFT shares on March 13th of that year, you would now have more than $1 million! That's a return on investment of more than 36,000 percent! Financial pundits always talk about finding the next Microsoft, but the fact is that they're probably looking in the wrong hemisphere. We know that the economies of China and the United States are headed in opposite directions—so which nation is more likely to produce the next great investment opportunity?

If you believe, as I do, that China is the answer, then we must become gurus on China. We must become, as Webster would say, "a person of knowledge and expertise." Later in this book I provide you with specific tools and resources, like the ones I have on my web site chinastockdigest.com. These are the same resources that have created tremendous profits for my private clients and for those who follow my China stock research. But for now, let's roll up our sleeves and learn about the industries and industrial centers in our world's new land of opportunity . . . the new capitalist China.

PART

II

CHINA'S ECONOMIC LANDSCAPE

CHAPTER 6

China's Booming
Base—Manufacturing

Being ignorant is not so much a shame as being unwilling to learn.

—Benjamin Franklin

The heart and soul of China's economic explosion is manufacturing. China may aspire to move up the labor-and-finished-goods value chain, but it will never fully abandon the basis of its economic success. Beijing has set its sights, instead, on expansion on every front.

From the sprawling factory complexes of Shenzhen to the cottage industries of the North, China has proven itself to be adept at finding a niche and filling it with astoundingly inexpensive manufactured goods. Most of us will remember the amazement we felt when brand new DVD players, which initially hit the market as thousand-dollar jewels of high technology suddenly began appearing in electronics stores and even groceries for as little as $30. It didn't take long for the machines to fly off from the shelves at those prices. Chinese manufacturing has shown the power to transform technology, to shape economies, and to change our own lives.

Building the Industrial Base

As we know, the low cost of labor has been one of the factors driving China's manufacturing competitiveness. The total average hourly labor cost in China is about $1, compared to an average of $30 per hour in the United States.[1] But there is much more to it than that. China is building more profitable industrial sectors, while clinging tenaciously to its hard-won manufacturing dominance.

China has at least 1.3 billion mouths to feed and some experts believe the real population of the country is substantially larger. The sheer numbers of people entering the job market every year, perhaps as many as 12 million, create a powerful competitive force that tends to hold wages in check. This relentless tide of job seekers also puts pressure on the central government to keep on expanding the manufacturing sector.

There's no disputing China's amazing success so far. Just over two decades ago, China's presence on the world stage as a manufacturer and exporter was absolutely tiny. The nation produced a paltry $8.7 billion worth of manufactured exports amounting to less than one percent of the world's total.[2] After decades of double-digit growth, China has become the world leader. Taking into account exports from Hong Kong and Taiwan, as well as mainland China, the Greater China industrial engine grabbed a 10 percent share of the world's manufacturing exports in 2004[3] and has continued to grow exponentially.

Manufactured goods now account for 89 percent of China's merchandise exports and an extraordinary 32 percent of the nation's GDP.[4] Half of China's fiscal revenue is generated by manufacturing and almost half of the urban working population of the nation works in manufacturing. Not since the emergence of the American industrial colossus in the late eighteenth and early nineteenth centuries has there been a phenomenon anything like it. The United States became the world's manufacturing leader by continuous innovation. U.S. manufacturers became dominant by creating the mass production line, by inventing new products, such as relatively inexpensive automobiles, and by implementing increasingly efficient production processes, including computer-controlled systems and industrial robots. China's manufacturing might is based on its manpower (and womanpower).

Who Transformed China?

A powerful combination of forces has come together in an entirely different way in China. The entrepreneurial spirit of Chinese businessmen (and women, who now rank among the nation's billionaires) is legendary, and the end of true communism unleashed a pent-up wave of capitalist forces. Deng Xiaoping's special economic zones drew upon the ambitions of expatriate Chinese throughout Asia, even though attracting new enterprises from Hong Kong was Deng's primary goal. Chinese students have gained advanced education and expertise at universities throughout the Western world, and, although many have chosen to stay in the countries where they got their education, millions have returned with expertise and an appetite for economic success.

One of the oddities of China's development is the number of small cities and towns that have become known for their specialties in particular manufacturing sectors. Haining, for example, a city of fewer than half a million people near Shanghai, has become a world-renowned source of leather goods. Most of Haining's 3,000 factories are involved in the production of leather products. A little farther from Shanghai, Taizhou has become the center of the plastic molding industry. In the Guangdong region, dozens of towns are known for their product specialties: toys in Chenghai, ceramics in Fengxi, motorcycles in Pengjinag, underwear in Yanbu, furniture in Dachong, and shoes in Pingzhou.[5] Chinese entrepreneurs have clearly been able to draw from locally developed skills and specialties imposed by former communist taskmasters to develop industries that are now so large that they sometimes satisfy a very high percentage of global demand. It speaks volumes about the aggressiveness of China's entrepreneurial drive that humble beginnings like state-owned factories and cottage industries have burgeoned into global forces.

The increasingly capitalist governments of China's regions and provinces, as well as Beijing, have taken pains to ensure that entrepreneurs have every advantage. In the past, banks were encouraged to lend money with abandon, and officials tended to look the other way when environmental regulations were broken. That is changing, but the government has many other tools at its disposal.

Why Foreign Business Can't Resist China

Foreign companies investing in a major manufacturing facility in certain parts of China pay no tax at all for as long as 20 years. Import duties and value-added taxes may also be waived. The land a manufacturing facility is built on may be provided free of charge. What's more, grants may be doled out to help train workers or to compensate the company for a generous portion of its capital investment.[6] Intel has been very secretive about the terms of its new $2.5 billion chipset manufacturing plant, but we can assume the incentives were generous. The incentives listed here certainly surpass anything available in the United States.

What's more, the money to build new facilities continues to pour in. China is second only to the United States as a recipient of foreign direct investment (FDI). Foreign investment in the United States tends to be liquid because it is often placed in stocks and bonds and can easily be withdrawn. Foreign direct investment in China is usually placed in factories and real estate. Although China has the lowest trade barriers of any developing country, it has tight restrictions on foreign investment in its internal stock markets.

The drive to attract new manufacturing concerns is so great that the government has added a slew of hidden subsidies, some of which are being contested as possible violations of World Trade Organization (WTO) rules to ensure fair competition. The cost of electricity is kept artificially low, the prices of other forms of energy, including coal and petroleum, are subject to price controls and subsidies to reduce the cost of shipping, and water is sold below its true value,[7] despite the fact that the nation is running desperately short of clean, fresh water supplies.

Manufacturing concerns in the West are coming to realize that they have little choice but to consider moving lock, stock, and barrel to China if they wish to survive. It's not just a question of matching the so-called China price demanded by major retailers like Wal-Mart. It's also a question of matching the competition. If a manufacturer's chief competitor is able to slash prices by moving operations to the Chinese mainland, any other company in the same field will be forced to take a long look at its chances of survival if it keeps its production facilities in a relatively high-wage Western country. In addition to all of the other incentives, there are other cost considerations, including an employer's freedom from health care obligations and possible labor union problems.

Becoming Number One

For U.S. industries like auto parts manufacturing and furniture making, the result has been a tailspin. American imports of Chinese-made furniture, for example, increased sixfold between 1996 and 2002, driven by deep price cuts by China-based factories. In a petition to the U.S. government, a coalition of 28 American furniture makers complained that their operating income had been slashed by 75 percent over two years,[8] and the industry faced possible collapse.

The United States remains a manufacturing colossus, but that sector's share of the U.S. economy is declining while Chinese industry aggressively takes up the slack. In July of 2007, China raced past a new economic milestone, becoming the number one source of exports to the United States. For decades, America's closest industrialized neighbor, Canada, jealously clung to its position as the number one exporter to the United States. But Canada finally fell behind when China sold $28.6 billion worth of goods to the United States in August of 2007, beating Canada by more than $4 billion.[9]

Although Chinese manufacturers often complain that their profit margins are being squeezed by U.S. buyers and international competitors with even lower wage structures, the evidence indicates that China is doing very well indeed. The textile industry faces the most intense cost-cutting pressures, but it is growing at a rate of 15 percent a year as measured by output value, profits, and exports, with a total output of $307 billion in 2006.[10] The industry is modernizing and raising productivity to keep ahead of foreign competitors. China's computer and home appliance sectors recorded massive profit increases during the first half of 2007. The Chinese *Xinhua* news agency boasts that computer enterprises enjoyed a 600 percent increase in profits, and home appliance companies rang up a 513 percent profit increase. The manufacturing profit boom extended through many sectors, with the nation's major steelmakers reporting earnings increases between 80 percent and 156 percent, due to increased demand, prices, and productivity.[11]

Chinese workers are not yet the most productive in the world. U.S. workers still hold that honor, partly because they work so many hours. But a survey by the International Labor Organization found that productivity was rising fastest in China and East Asia. Average annual productivity growth was 2.1 percent in the industrialized world compared to a stunning 8.5 percent in Asia. In fact, China's exports are growing so quickly that the government has repealed some of the tax incentives given to energy-intensive and pollution-producing industries that manufacture 2,200 products.

Tomorrow's Manufacturing Giants

Where does it all end? Despite the nation's breakneck pace of growth, one of China's top scientific institutions says the economy won't be transformed from an agricultural into an industrial economy until 2015.[12] China is going full speed ahead.

Looking to the future, Chinese industries are reaching out to become global players. The IBM Institute for Business Value says 60 Chinese firms will join the ranks of well-known multinationals in the next decade.[13] Here's a list of 12 firms to watch as Chinese manufacturing takes on a global presence: BaoSteel, Haier Appliances, Lenovo Computers, Hisense Home Electronics, Midea Group Appliances, SVT Group Electronics, Younger Textiles, CHINT Electronics, Wahaha Beverages, Skyworth Home Electronics, People Electric Appliance Group, and Aux Group Appliances.

Watch those names. IBM says they are the companies with the potential to be the next Sony or Samsung or IBM.

7

China's Auto Industry—In Full Gear

*Capital as such is not evil; it is its wrong use that is evil. Capital
in some form or other will always be needed.*

—Mohandas K. Gandhi

The biggest car-buying boom in history is happening right now
in China. The people of China have fallen in love with automobile
ownership in a big way and they are creating a massive industry to
satisfy domestic demand and eventually to supply the world.

The Chinese love affair with the automobile is reminiscent of
the United States' own romance with the car. Auto ownership is a
symbol of success, independence, and mobility. Sales of automobiles continue to boom because customers continue to buy the largest and most luxurious vehicle they can afford. Commutes are slow
and getting slower every month, but still Chinese workers prefer
driving to work over public transit even though major cities are
scrambling to add miles of subway lines and fielding fleets of spar-
kling new buses.

Full Speed Ahead

Since the turn of the century, sales have been increasing at a rate of
at least 25 percent every year, with annual sales figures approaching
ten million vehicles.[1] In 2006, China raced past Japan to become

the world's second-largest market for new vehicles, with total sales of 7.2 million units.[2] Only the United States buys more automobiles than China and many economists predict that the U.S. record won't stand forever. Americans currently own an estimated 226 million vehicles. By 2025, China's total car ownership is expected to surpass that number and continue to increase exponentially. The Chinese economy has broken every speed limit set for it in the past and it wouldn't be surprising to see China become number one much sooner.

As discussed in Chapter 4, Beijing has established national goals to limit energy consumption and reduce pollution. Paradoxically, the government is also doing everything it can to build a car culture and a car industry that will rival the United States. Although approximately 15,000 miles of highways are already completed, the government is pushing ahead with the construction of more roadways. For example, a huge national highway system that is 52,800 miles long, is under construction. When completed, the Chinese network of roads and highways will be approximately the same length as all of the interstates built in the United States since the 1950s. It apparently matters little to bureaucrats that streets and highways become more clogged every year and smog fills the air in cities like Beijing. What seems to matter more is further developing the auto industry so that it can be the largest in the world.

Despite the crowding on the roads, the growth of auto ownership in China has a long way to go by world standards. Twenty-seven people out of every thousand in China currently own a car. According to the *Xinhua* news agency, the world's average level of vehicle ownership is 150 units for every 1,000 people.

Take note of this sobering fact before you consider driving a car in China. According to the Ministry of Public Security, the number of experienced drivers in China is estimated at about 73 percent. What makes for an experienced driver? More than three years of experience behind the wheel. That means millions and millions of drivers that we might consider novices are engaged in urban warfare for room to move on swarming city streets. Auto accidents account for an appalling 650 deaths and 45,000 injuries daily, making China the most dangerous driving environment in the world.[3] A Beijing traffic cop has a life expectancy of only 45 years, partly due to air pollution levels.

Automakers Battle for Position

China's relentless increase in new car sales indicates that the nation's demand is far from being satisfied. According to the powerful National Development and Reform Commission (NDRC), the car ownership ratio will rise to 40 vehicles for every 1,000 people by 2010.[4] The NDRC also predicts that 55 million vehicles will be swarming over China's roads by 2010. As a result of the increased number of cars and trucks on the roads, officials optimistically predict that the nation's gasoline consumption will rise by no more than 50 percent because of increasing engine efficiency.

An astonishing number of vehicle manufacturers have sprung up to fill the voracious public demand. There seems to be no general agreement on the total number of carmakers in China, with estimates ranging from 100 to 150. The situation is reminiscent of the early years of automobile manufacturing in the United States, when dozens of ambitious companies leaped into the business, only to go bankrupt or be swallowed up by the conglomerates that would eventually become known as the Big Three.

If it's difficult to keep up with the number of Chinese auto manufacturers, it's even more difficult to keep track of the number of models. In 2005, a record number of new models, 105 varieties, hit the market and production began to exceed demand. The NDRC says production capacity has risen above 10 million units annually and new models are still pouring into showrooms from Beijing to Tibet.

As the market grows, foreign automakers have been struggling to increase their market share through joint ventures with the biggest Chinese manufacturers. After the first, trouble-plagued joint venture between American Motors Corporation (which was later taken over by Chrysler) and Beijing Jeep in 1983, the government realized that stronger measures were needed. By 1991, a mere 81,000 cars were being produced by the entire industry, but the growth curve was about to take off with 25 percent increases in production and sales every year.[5]

Beijing had decided that automobile manufacturing was to become a national *pillar* industry and the world's automakers rushed in to take part in what they expected to be a gold rush. After Beijing Jeep, Volkswagen rushed in to become China's leading brand through joint ventures called Shanghai Auto Industries—Volkswagen,

First Auto Works—Volkswagen. Other multinational joint ventures followed, including Shanghai Auto Industries—General Motors, Chang'An—Ford, Chang'An—Suzuki, Guangzhou Automobile Group—Honda, Donfeng-Nissan, Donfeng-Kia, Donfeng-Citroen, Beijing-Hyundai, Chery-Chrysler, Chery-Fiat, Brilliance China Automotive—BMW, and Guangzhou Automobile Group—Toyota.

The crowd of national and international automakers competing for the Chinese automobile market has sparked a price war, forcing most manufacturers to offer price cuts. But internal demand has been so great that the industry giants have still managed to report extraordinary profit increases. For example, the car industry as a whole reported a 65 percent jump in profits for the first half of 2007, clearing a total income of $4 billion.[6] One of China's independent car companies, Chery, recorded the biggest profit increase among the majors, with growth of 210 percent.

Best Sellers

The best-selling models in China are hybrids from joint ventures. The top five models are the Volkswagen Jetta, the Volkswagen Santana, the Buick Excelle, Toyota's Camry, and Chery's famous QQ.

Chery is also joining up with foreign companies to compete in overseas markets. China's most successful independent car company has struck an agreement with the Chrysler Group to assemble small, inexpensive cars in China for export under the Dodge brand name. Chery is also working on a deal with Fiat and Alfa Romeo. Another independent, Geely, hopes to have a model in U.S. showrooms before 2010. Brilliance China Automotive, a BMW partner, may have a car in U.S. showrooms even sooner.

Chery is already a major exporter of its own models. Sales abroad for 2007 are in the 100,000 range, with China's total auto exports exceeding 500,000.[7] Current exports are to less developed nations such as Brazil, Uruguay, Egypt, Ukraine, and countries in Africa. Not wanting to repeat the fiasco of Yugoslavia's failed Yugo automobile in North America, Chinese brands are gaining experience in the Third World before attacking more critical markets.

Before exporting completed automobiles, China had already taken an aggressive stance in the auto parts industry. China has raced ahead of Germany to become the second-largest exporter of car parts to the United States. Japan remains the number one exporter of parts, but Chinese companies are not standing still. Chinese firms like Wonder Auto Technology and Wanxiang are buying U.S. plants so they can access U.S. technology and markets. Chinese manufacturers are beating even Mexican auto parts factories through lower costs for labor, raw materials, and the low value of the Chinese yuan.

Many of the partners in joint ventures are at least partly owned by provincial governments in China, with a percentage of shares being offered on the Shanghai and Hong Kong exchanges. Brilliance China Automotive Holdings Ltd. (CBA) is one of the first and still one of the few automotive enterprises to be offered as an ADR in the United States.

Direct investment in automotive enterprises through the Shanghai stock exchange is still off-limits to most foreigners. Investment on the Hong Kong exchange is almost as difficult to manage, unless one invests through a growing variety of funds, as we see later in this book.

For the time being, the industry is in something of a shakedown phase, as a surplus of manufacturers engage in cutthroat pricing to win market share. For the time being, it remains difficult for investors to pick the probable winners in China's automotive boom and own shares directly in those companies. Ownership of shares in resource suppliers, parts suppliers, and major energy firms will likely be the safer bet until the industry's dominant players emerge and offer more ADRs in the United States or shares become available through mutual funds and exchange-traded funds in Hong Kong.

Investors who own U.S. and European automotive stocks should also keep an eye on the progress of joint ventures with Western companies to stay aware of who is winning the race for dominance on China's roads and which company will reap substantial future profits from the growing auto export market.

Tomorrow's Global Giants

China is ultimately destined to take its place on the world stage, just as Japanese and South Korean automakers have done. They will be a competitive group and three of those mentioned in this chapter are projected to be industry leaders. The IBM Institute for Business Value says a total of five companies in the motor vehicle industry have the potential to become global players. They are SAIC, Chery, and Geely in the auto manufacturing field and Wanxiang in auto parts and Lifan in motorcycles.

Look for these brand names to follow in the footsteps of Toyota, Nissan, Hyundai, and Kia. The Chinese are closing in quickly in our rearview mirrors.

8

China's Energy Industry—Red Hot

He that waits upon fortune is never sure of a dinner.
—Benjamin Franklin

If you still think the China story doesn't amount to much beyond a few *Made in China* labels at your local Wal-Mart, think again. Think back to the last time you pumped gas and try to remember how much lower your gas bill was just three years ago. Anyone who has recently taken a road trip can tell you that the price of oil has never been higher. And from one investment guru to another, let me just tell you that the price of gas is not going to drop dramatically for an extended period ever again. Never.

China's voracious thirst for oil and energy, along with the growing demand for oil imports in other developing nations, is a world-changing event. Far beyond the momentary sticker shock we all feel at the gas pumps, competition for energy supplies is transforming the global economy, the environment, and the political arena. Expensive energy has boosted the profit margins of multinational oil giants so dramatically that howls of protest have been heard from vocal and powerful critics in the United States and abroad. The search for new energy sources has set off territorial disputes for drilling rights under the Arctic ice cap, resulting in international disputes among Russian, U.S., Canadian, and other northern powers. Moreover, the environmental consequences of the energy boom will become an unavoidable bone of contention as green-house gas emissions continue to soar.

Why is it all happening so quickly? In a word: China. The growth in demand for energy in China is so rapid that it boggles the imagination. Total energy consumption in this nation of 1.3 billion has risen by an average of 11 percent every year for the past five years.[1] Taking into account China's booming demand for all forms of energy, the nation is increasing its power consumption by an amount equivalent to that of a country the size of England every year. Some analysts say the rate of energy expansion is even greater.

China's Insatiable Appetite

Seventy percent of China's energy consumption depends on the nation's ample reserves of coal. Demand for coal-powered electricity rose by a remarkable 90 gigawatts in 2006. In more comprehensible terms, China's power grid added the equivalent of two large coal-fired generating stations every week.[2] Two new power plants a week! The equivalent of 104 new coal-burning plants per year! On the global energy scene, nothing on this scale has ever happened before.

So, to those who say China's presence on the world energy scene hasn't yet touched Western oil prices, I can only reply, "Rubbish!" Oil prices are adjusting not only in accordance with existing demand, but also in anticipation of future supply shortages. OPEC claims to be raising its output to satisfy global energy needs, but it has not so far been enough to keep pace with the incredible demand surge from China and East Asia.

China will be assigned much of the blame as worldwide energy supplies hit a major crunch in the coming decade. But keep in mind that developing nations are also increasing their energy consumption. Developed countries, including many Asian economic powerhouses like Japan, Taiwan, and South Korea have offloaded many of their energy-intensive industries to China. Offshoring of industrial infrastructure adds to Chinese energy demand, but it hasn't done much to dampen the thirst for oil in the countries that sent their industries abroad. Most Western nations continue to increase their own consumption of imported oil every year despite pious pronouncements about the importance of conservation.

During the 1990s, China was actually an oil exporter. But those days are long, long gone. During 2007, China passed a sobering milestone. The country's imports of crude oil exceeded domestic production for the first time in its history. With more than 50 percent of China's oil supplies now coming from other countries, the economic and political implications are obviously global. The United States is on a collision course. Competition with China for energy resources is about to become a good deal more intense, but for the time being, the new energy picture barely appears on the American public's radar screen.

Where and when will it end? Not anytime soon. China's imports of crude leaped by an unprecedented 14.4 percent in 2006 and were on track to exceed 10 percent for 2007.[3] Double-digit increases in oil imports have been a reality for years and are not likely to ease unless a price squeeze or a supply crunch changes the behaviors of Chinese consumers and consumers worldwide. For the time being, newly wealthy Chinese drivers are buying gas-guzzling SUVs and other energy hogs with almost as much abandon as U.S. consumers. Chinese industries use 20 to 100 percent more energy per unit of output compared to their American and Japanese counterparts, according to the World Bank. Inefficient though it may be, energy-hungry Chinese industries continue to expand relentlessly.

Building Up Reserves of Energy

Adding to the sharp energy demand curve is the awareness that China is building its first strategic petroleum reserve. Much like the U.S. reserve, China's four strategic reserve stations are being prepared to supply the nation through periods of domestic crisis and international shortages without disrupting the domestic economy or the lives of Chinese citizens. When the tanks are filled, presumably by 2012, China should have enough oil in reserve to carry the nation through a 30-day supply crunch. Buying the oil needed to fill the tanks is expected to add as much as 2 percent to the annual growth rate of crude imports.[4] Predicting the end of demand from China's strategic reserve is impossible because the government is attempting to time its purchases to coincide with dips in international prices.

Nothing depicts the story of China's red-hot energy sector more vividly than a comparison between ExxonMobil and Sinopec.

During 2006, ExxonMobil, the world's largest publicly traded company, hired 149 supertankers to ferry oil around the globe, mostly to American consumers. This private navy was the largest the world had ever seen, at least until China came into the picture. Now Asia's largest oil refiner, China Petroleum & Chemical Corporation, known as Sinopec (SNP), is hiring more supertankers than ExxonMobil to haul oil from Angola and Venezuela as well as other international destinations.[5] In addition to the impressive number of supertankers in the Sinopec fleet, the company is sharply increasing the number of ships being leased. In 2005, Sinopec hired only 86 ships. In 2006, more than 100 vessels were hired for single voyages. In 2007, the number raced past the 150 mark. Of course, Sinopec is only one of several major Chinese oil companies actively seeking foreign sources of oil.

China is also scrambling to discover and exploit more sources of oil domestically. The country's biggest and oldest reserve, the Daqing field, is in steep decline despite intensive efforts to boost production with modern extraction technologies. Important new reserves have been discovered in Bohai Bay and farther out into the South China Sea. But China's National Bureau of Statistics, which strives to avoid painting gloomy pictures, reported that national oil production rose only 2 percent in 2006, while the economy grew by more than 11 percent.[6] In the month before the Bureau made the report, May of 2007, oil imports jumped by a grossly disproportionate 23 percent.

Domestic coal production is rising, too, but not nearly fast enough. A 7 percent increase in coal production during the first half of 2007 brought national output to more than a billion tons for the period. But it seems the nation's biggest energy resource just can't keep pace with demand. Once again, China is being transformed from being a net exporter of coal to an aggressive importer. Companies like Yanzhou Coal (YZC) have become partners in the development of major mines abroad like the giant Austar coal mine in New South Wales, Australia.

The search for more oil sources, meanwhile, has taken China to many countries that the United States considers unsavory. Among the dictatorships and backwaters of the world, China's biggest supplier is Angola, followed by Saudi Arabia, Iran, and Russia. The Chinese are also currently forging deals with the likes of Sudan and Myanmar (formerly known as Burma). China's oil companies also have interests in 20 African countries, including Libya, Algeria, and Ethiopia. Pursuing these oil sources is a high-risk strategy that is guaranteed to alienate many Western powers that are competing for oil supplies, but consider many of China's energy partners to be pariahs at best, and a danger to world peace in the case of Iran.

Electrifying the Future

Finding more oil and digging more coal will never provide the long-term solutions that China needs to maintain its energy growth curve and prevent future electricity shortages. According to *Xinhua*, China's electric power capacity was boosted tenfold over the past three decades, but that still isn't enough. With more than 500 million kilowatts of power on the nation's power grid in 2006, state officials were confident that this unprecedented reserve would prevent brownouts that year. They were wrong. According to the State Electricity Regulatory Commission (SERC), power consumption increased faster than the growth of the economy, up more than 15 percent in the first half of 2007. The situation has become so pressing that Beijing has now opened a strategic asset, the nation's power grid, to foreign investors in hopes of improving its notoriously poor efficiency and preventing electricity shortages.

In an effort to diversify supplies and find cleaner sources of electric power, alternative forms of energy, including solar, wind, and other renewable sources of power, are being developed. Hydroelectric power projects are being built in increasingly remote areas of the country, but there are no new equivalents of the massive Three Gorges Dam in the works. More immediately, natural gas is being tapped as an energy source for the future. Large new reserves have been discovered in China, and major terminals are being built in coastal regions to receive liquefied natural gas (LNG) ships from suppliers in Australia and farther afield. Coal-bed methane from the nation's vast coalfields is another promising source, as is coal liquefaction, a technology that converts coal into gasoline.

Nuclear generating stations are an attractive alternative for generating large amounts of electricity, with low immediate impact on the nation's pollution crisis. Westinghouse has signed a long-awaited, multibillion-dollar contract to build four nuclear power stations for China. Under the guidance of Westinghouse's new parent, Toshiba of Japan, the American company will hand over the technology for its most advanced reactors. French and Russian reactor builders are also working on contracts to build nuclear power stations in China. A total of 32 new reactors are expected to come online before 2020. But, in another sobering measure of China's insatiable energy demand, nuclear power is not expected to furnish more than 4 percent of the nation's electricity by the 2020 construction deadline.

Energy efficiency and energy conservation are essential to preventing severe shortages in the future. Sounding somewhat desperate, the NDRC announced in late 2007 that investments amounting to an almost unimaginable 10 percent of national GDP would be required to get the necessary renewable energy projects underway. The powerful government agency is welcoming foreign partners. Meanwhile, the most effective way of improving energy supplies—conserving them—is taking root in a country not accustomed to energy efficiency. Tax policies are being implemented by the government to force large and wasteful energy consumers to cut back. The big opportunity for the future is in promoting energy efficiency and proving renewable sources of energy. Those are the better mousetraps that China needs desperately to prevent major shortages in coming decades.

Companies providing solar energy equipment to the world, such as Suntech Power (STP), have been among China's best performing internationally traded stocks. Oil exploration and refining companies like Sinopec (SNP), PetroChina (PTR), and China National Offshore Oil Corporation (CEO) have also performed very well on stock markets and they outstrip many Western competitors in the global search for new oil supplies.

China's Bonanza— Banking and Finance

A bank is a place that will lend you money if you can prove that you don't need it.

—Bob Hope

Depending on when you last checked their balance sheets, China's biggest banks are either basket cases or superstars. In fact, there seemed to be little hope for the survival of China's entire banking industry during the early years of the capitalist revolution. But today, Chinese and foreign investors are creating a financial system that will certainly become a powerful international force, a development that once seemed extremely remote.

Avoiding a Financial Crisis

Long before the Chinese economic miracle became a twenty-first century phenomenon, the nation's banking system was notorious for the lackluster and inefficient management of its own finances. China's major national banks were often referred to as *policy banks* because they had the unenviable task of carrying out financial policies that were dictated by the government. These economic strategies and procedures often made little financial sense. For example, the Beijing government mandated that its agricultural, commercial, merchant, and industrial banks lend out enormous amounts of money to failing state enterprises with little hope that the money would ever be paid back. Most people would call these absurd loans losses, but in the banking world they go by the more polite name of *nonperforming loans,* or NPLs. (Calling a deadbeat's worthless paper a nonperforming loan makes it sound more like a high-performance automobile with a repairable engine problem, rather than a total financial loss for which somebody might have to be blamed.)

The issuance of nonperforming loans created a financial crisis that threatened to ground China's fledgling market economy. Although a number of authors have suggested that the problem was bad enough to spark a global financial panic, the scale of China's nonperforming loan crisis has never been fully revealed. Yet, many economists believe that the issuing and spending of nonperforming loans was a problem that involved many different groups, not just the government. Although moribund state industries took money without the slightest intention of paying it back, bureaucrats and corrupt middlemen who ordered billions to be paid out were also to blame for this financial disaster. Also, bank officials who meekly provided these outrageous loans and did not enforce repayment are also to blame. Some of China's biggest banks became known as *state-owned basket cases.*

Although China's gargantuan nonperforming loan problem has not been solved, it is no longer considered to be a financial crisis. Once estimated to be more than 23 percent of the banking industry's assets, NPLs had been reduced to 8.98 percent by the end of June 2007.[1] Among the major Chinese banks currently listed on Asian stock exchanges, some nonperforming loan ratios have fallen below 2 percent. This diminishing number of NPLs has been essential to the nation's economic health.

The Banking Transformation

What happened in China during the twenty-first century is one of the great financial revivals of our time. A combination of foreign direct investment and the offshoring of industries established the industrial base that ultimately sparked the Chinese banking engine into life. According to Alfred Yeung of Ernst and Young, "The extent to which that nation's banking assets are now public is a truly remarkable feat and underscores the [government's] commitment to reform in the banking sector."[2] Banks, which were once thought of as "zombies" or "basket cases," grew tenfold in just four years. The China Banking Regulatory Commission (CBRC) estimated that the total assets of the banking sector totaled $5.78 trillion in 2006, with profits of $53 billion.[3] State-owned commercial banks raked in a return on equity of 14.9 percent.

Another arm of China's financial services sector, the securities industry, is also booming, partly as a result of bank stock listings. In October 2006, the Industrial and Commercial Bank of China set a world record with its $21.9 billion initial public offering. Profits at securities dealers, once beset by losses, stock market stagnation, and accusations of corruption, soared during 2007 as China's internal stock markets set one record high after another. The *Shanghai Securities News* reports that the combined net profits of 23 mainland-listed brokerages rose by 425 percent during the first half of 2007.[4] As the Chinese securities industry recovers from a multiyear slump, foreign firms will be permitted to invest in mainland brokerages.

China's biggest banks have completed their reforms and gone public, joining the ranks of the world's top 10. The Bank of China and China Construction Bank are numbers six and seven, respectively on the list of the world's top 10 banking institutions as measured by assets.[5] Earnings are booming among the major listed banks and among smaller regional firms. While Industrial and Commercial Bank (ICBC) brought in earnings of almost $5 billion during the first half of 2007, up approximately 50 percent, China Merchants Bank took in $736 million, an increase of 100 percent in profits. Industrial Bank showed profit growth of almost 90 percent, while China Citic Bank and China Minsheng Bank generated profit increases of 80 percent and 60 percent respectively.

As Chinese share prices have escalated, Industrial and Commercial Bank has risen to become the world's largest bank by market capitalization with a value of $254 billion. That exceeds Citigroup's market cap by $3 billion and puts ICBC far ahead of the third-place contender, HSBC Holdings, which has a market cap of just $215 billion.[6] To some degree, ICBC's success reflects stock market conditions in China and a high degree of government ownership through nontradable shares more than the intrinsic value of the bank. Citigroup took in revenue of $90 billion in 2007, almost four times the earnings of ICBC.

Improving the processes and efficiencies of Chinese banks was by no means a cheap or easy task. Nouriel Roubini, of New York University, estimates that the Chinese government injected a whopping half trillion dollars into the banking system to stabilize the sector and prepare major banks for stock exchange listings.[7] However, the rescue isn't over yet. In 2007, one of the big four state-owned banks, the Agricultural Bank of China, remained unlisted and received a capital bailout of $40 billion. The Agricultural Bank of China suffered an especially severe burden of bad loans because it had been tasked to support a difficult and often unprofitable sector of the economy. Beijing is also preparing a second round of loan bailouts, starting with a $20 billion capital injection into the Commercial Development Bank using its huge foreign exchange reserves.

Chinese banks had to get their houses fully in order by 2007 because the nation's financial sector was being opened up to foreign competition under the terms of China's accession to membership in the World Trade Organization. Seventy-one foreign banks were operating in China before the 2007 deadline, but most had been limited to dealing in foreign currency transactions. At the time this book was published, nine major multinational banks had applied for retail licenses, which will give them access to China's huge pool of savings, estimated at more than $4 trillion.[8] The foreign banks incorporated to do retail business in China are Citigroup of the United States, the Bank of East Asia and Hang Seng Bank of Hong Kong, HSBC and Standard Chartered of Britain, Mizuho Corporate Bank and Sumitomo Mitsui Bank of Japan, ABN Amro Holdings NV of the Netherlands, and DBS Bank of Singapore.

Our Piece of the Action

We are witnessing the development of an important symbiotic relationship between Chinese banks and their foreign partners. Most foreign banks are aware that they cannot establish branches throughout China because of the cost and logistical complexity of such a vast undertaking. For the most part, they must rely on a nationwide network of native Chinese banks to establish a presence throughout the country. In the resulting symbiotic relationship, foreign banks work with Chinese branches and banks by providing financial services that the Chinese are unable to provide. China's major banks realize that they do not have the expertise or the experience required to compete effectively in modern consumer banking. Therefore, they tend to rely on their foreign partners for help in providing services such as credit cards, ATM machines, remittances, and various forms of retail lending.

China's policy banks also need help dealing with the needs of modern business clients. Sophisticated banking services, including equipment leasing, corporate financial restructuring, and international consulting, are essential for Chinese industries seeking to establish a global presence. As a result, joint ventures and equity purchase agreements are being established between Chinese and foreign banks to give both parties in international operations a financial stake in a successful outcome. One of the pioneers in the field of joint ventures is Bank of America Corporation, which paid $3 billion for a 9 percent stake in China Construction Bank in 2005.[9]

The Bank of America–China Construction Bank deal has been fruitful for both sides. Bank of America has also been able to team up with the China Construction Bank in joint ownership of a major leasing venture aimed at the power generation and rail industries. What's more, Bank of America's purchase price for its 9 percent equity stake looks like a bargain in view of CCB's September 2007 IPO on the Shanghai exchange, which raised $7.7 billion for just 3.85 percent of the Chinese bank's expanded share capital.

Not all partnerships between Chinese and Western banks are harmonious, but foreign operations are generating substantial profits. A report from the *Chinese Securities Journal* says profit growth tripled at Citigroup, ABN Amro, and other foreign banks after they were allowed to offer local currency services. In total, overseas banks earned $401 million in the first five months of 2007, an increase of 43 percent from the same period a year earlier.[10] Foreign banks have opened 186 outlets in 25 Chinese cities, targeting high net worth individuals who are looking for improved customer service and are impressed by the international reputation of foreign banks. China's national banks operate approximately 10,000 branches each, but the China Banking Research Center says foreign-funded banks have enjoyed rapid profit growth with their experience in serving small and medium enterprises, private banking, and the securities industry.[11]

As foreign financial giants reach into China, Chinese banks are also reaching out to the world. China Development Bank is participating in the biggest global investment ever made by a Chinese bank, and attempted to invest as much as $13.5 billion in a complex transaction involving Britain's Barclays Bank and its Dutch rival, ABN Amro. China's leading banks are also applying to set up branches in the United States, serving American branches of Chinese companies.

During the first half of 2007, foreign insurance companies have been relatively slow to establish positions in China, with 45 companies from 15 countries taking in premiums of $2.11 billion.[12] The China Insurance Regulatory Commission believes that domestic insurers can learn from foreign companies' experience in risk control, corporate governance, and product development. The potential market is huge for companies that can establish a presence through the vast branch network of domestic operators.

Banking on the Future

It is no exaggeration to say that every aspect of China's financial industry is on a steep trajectory to achieve world-class status. Standard Chartered plc believes that China could become its largest market for private banking in just 10 years.[13] The global accountancy giant Deloitte Touche Tohmatsu expects that China will become its largest market as measured by staff and revenues in approximately 20 years.

The future seems limitless in a market as large as China's. The Chinese stock market is already bigger than that of Japan. The Chinese financial services industry, however, is not meeting the needs of consumers. Although foreign institutions are restricted from gaining majority ownership in China's financial institutions, they are facing the greatest investment management opportunity in the world through joint ventures. As the Chinese middle class becomes ever larger and more sophisticated, insurers, brokers, bankers, and financial advisers will discover an increasingly wealthy customer base, numbering in the hundreds of millions.

China's banks have so far chosen not to list on U.S. stock exchanges as ADRs, but a stake in them is available to investors through the mutual funds and exchange-traded funds described in the concluding chapters of this book.

CHAPTER 10

China's Communications Revolution—Almost Free Speech

An investment in knowledge pays the best interest.
—Benjamin Franklin

North Americans like to imagine they've undergone an entirely unique communications revolution over the past 10 years, fast-forwarding into the twenty-first century with innovations including wireless Internet access, cellular and satellite telephones, and hybrid devices like Blackberries and iPhones. But the speed of change in the United States has been minor compared to the communications revolution underway in China. Truly, the pace of progress China has achieved in the communications arena is nothing short of breathtaking.

The Ultimate Communications Device

During the same hyperactive decade that most of us marvel at, the Chinese people have jumped an entire *century* in their communications abilities. When Deng Xiaoping first exhorted his countrymen to go ahead and get rich, the dial telephone was the most advanced communications tool available and the vast majority of Chinese homes couldn't afford one. Even the privileged families that could manage to pay for a telephone had to wait years for service.

China now has more than half a trillion cellular telephones. If this isn't a revolution, nothing else qualifies. To be exact, the total number of handsets exceeded 600 million in late 2007, according to the Ministry of Information. This number continues to grow exponentially. Every month another five million subscribers sign up for instantaneous cell phone service. Pause a moment to consider that—five million new subscribers every month, when just a few years ago, the residents of China couldn't even afford telephones!

What is equally notable about the communications phenomenon is that the products China provides are of optimal quality and incorporate the most innovative technology. For example, the voice quality and data transfer capabilities of the Chinese cell phone providers surpass anything we currently have available in the United States. I know from my own personal experience. As one of the 600 million cell phone users in China, the service I get from China Mobile when using my personal cell phone in Shanghai is far superior and quite a bit less expensive than anything I can get from a cell phone company in the United States. When I am in China, I can use my cell phone on an elevator or even while I am on the subway— and I always get perfect reception. Try doing that in New York or San Francisco. Moreover, if I need to make more calls, I can recharge my cell phone account at any newsstand. Also, unlike my U.S. service plan, my Chinese plan does not have an associated monthly service fee. Certainly, China has made it easier to "reach out and touch someone" than we have done in the United States.

Just 30 years ago, China had made very few strides from the days of Alexander Graham Bell. Today, there are twice as many Chinese cell phone users as there are people in the United States. The number of subscribers, who sign up for monthly service, would make up a contingent of customers large enough to support an entire communications company in the United States. The trend is still accelerating, and that, in my mind, counts as a world-scale communications revolution.

The nation's two giant cell phone companies are China Mobile (CHL) and China Unicom (CHU). China Mobile is by far the larger. These companies earned their superior status by monopolizing the competition and setting up user-friendly features that brought in extra revenue. It goes without saying that these two telephone companies are majority state-owned enterprises, but that does not mean they haven't performed exceptionally well for buyers of their ADRs.

Handsets, which enable a person to do more than just talk on the phone, are one option that appeals to the Chinese communications consumer, while generating high revenues for the cellular phone companies. Chinese city dwellers consider their mobile telephones a necessity of life. Handsets are used for much more than a quick chat or maybe a photograph. They are, instead, typically used for business or to surf the Web. For example, during the onset of a recent typhoon in Shanghai, a Chinese friend of mine was busy looking up storm tracks from AccuWeather online from his tiny handheld phone.

Text messaging is another feature that provides extra revenue for mobile phone companies. The Chinese are very uncomfortable with the idea of leaving messages when they can't get through. Who knows when someone might get around to listening to your urgent message if they had to hunt through their voice mail? Who else might hear your private message? That's why texting is an essential skill in China, not just an idle diversion for Western teenagers. Texting puts your urgent communication (and they are all urgent in today's China) on the screen of your intended target without a nanosecond of delay. Cell phones also generate revenue streams from downloads of ringtones, wallpaper, games, and other enhancements.

A slew of NASDAQ-listed companies sprang up to sell these services to the nation's cohort of 600 million cell phone users and they have performed very well for several years. But China Mobile and China Unicom have crushed the profit streams of a number of these smaller firms by muscling into their territory and shutting added-value providers out of their revenue stream as much as possible.

Revenues collected from China's cell phone users are considerably lower than averages in the Western world. Right now, the name of the game is market penetration, and China Mobile (CHL) is the leader by a country mile. As market penetration begins to saturate China's main cities, cell phone providers are reaching out to the countryside. Penetration in rural areas is estimated at roughly 25 percent of the available market. Inexpensive monochromatic phones and low-cost service contracts are being offered to attract isolated rural subscribers.

That means hundreds of millions of cell phones have yet to be sold in China and just as many service contracts are waiting to be signed. The Chinese cell phone industry does lag in the production of handsets, but it is gearing up to compete with the likes of Nokia, Samsung, Motorola, and Ericsson. Although foreign brands dominate 70 percent of the Chinese cell phone market, the consulting firm China Center for Information Industry Development Consulting predicts that China is on track to produce 500 million cell phones annually.[1]

The Wired World

Fixed-line telephones are largely controlled by two major state-owned enterprises, China Telecom (CHA) and China Netcom (CN). In Taiwan, Chungwha Telecom (CHT) is the biggest player in both fields, and a very nice dividend payer in the island's more static telephony market.

The mainland's fixed-line operators are working against some big disadvantages. Cell phones have come to dominate the market partly because service is easily and almost instantly available. Fixed-line phones require countless miles of copper wire to link every phone in every home in every city. This kind of network is something that has evolved over time in the developed world. But hooking up the entire Chinese nation with hardwired phone service in the space of just a few years would have been an unimaginably large logistical undertaking.

Cell phone networks have proven to be much easier to set up, requiring just a few towers here and there to serve vast numbers of people. Building a robust network of cellular towers and microwave transmission links in the most remote parts of the country has proven to be a problem that the Chinese communications industry has mastered very nimbly. Long before copper wires could reach every village and home, cell telephones have captured much of the available market.

That doesn't mean there's a lack of business opportunities for fixed-line operators like China Netcom and China Unicom. Even though increasing numbers of subscribers are migrating to cellular service, they still share a market of 370 million users.[2] The two companies are rapidly expanding their broadband services to most of the Chinese mainland, where a huge market opportunity still awaits them. The number of broadband users in China is growing so quickly that demand for service will soon surpass that of the

United States. According to the research firm Ovum, there should be at least 79 million broadband subscribers in China by the end of 2007, surpassing the United States and making it the world's largest broadband market.[3] Broadband use is projected to continue growing with an anticipated 139 million subscribers online by 2010.

The next step is broadband telephony using 3G and 4G (third generation and fourth generation technology) systems. China insists that these systems be developed domestically, probably to fend off foreign rivals and to enhance domestic intelligence-gathering capabilities in wireless communications. Political stability is always a consideration in the new China, right alongside profitability.

The Internet Revolution

By broadband, by cell phone, or by a stolen moment at a cyber café, the Internet has become a hugely popular means of communication among the Chinese people, especially among well-educated, prosperous males. Once again, China is catching up with the United States in the Internet revolution. With at least 150 million citizens already online, and an average annual growth rate of 8 percent, the Chinese Information Ministry predicts there will be more than 200 million Internet users by 2010. Like so many government predictions, this forecast is probably conservative.

The Chinese communications revolution is already generating impressive amounts of money. The sector's value is projected to expand at a rate of 15 percent annually, generating revenues of $337 billion by 2010. According to the Ministry's calculations, this projection will amount to a remarkable 10 percent of China's GDP.[4] Revenues from the digital publishing industry have already risen above $2.5 billion per year. Internet advertising, still in its infancy, brought in $640 million in 2006. Custom ring tones, games, and animations for cell phones generated a billion dollars. Internet periodicals and books brought in almost $100 million.

Game-playing on the Internet with multiple participants is enormously popular and profitable, generating an anticipated $1.3 billion in 2007. The sector is China's largest Internet segment and it is expected to expand at a rate of 11 percent a year until 2017.[5] Participation in multiple user games has become so popular that it has raised alarm among the mandarins of Beijing, who regard it as something of a dangerous addiction for the nation's youth.

China's Internet industry has also developed its own very successful versions of Google and eBay. China's homegrown search engine, Baidu (BIDU) has outpaced Google. Alibaba has modeled its e-commerce offering to appeal to uniquely Chinese tastes, beating eBay in the Internet auction business through taobao.com and providing B2B services internationally through Alibaba web sites. Amazon.com has pledged to expand its investment in online retailing in hopes of beating its Chinese rival, dangdang.com. So far dangdang.com is beating Amazon's Chinese portal, joyo.com, but the online retail business is still in its infancy among China's fledgling Internet users and the fight for dominance is too close to call. Among China's listed Internet companies, valuations tend to be extremely high and earnings among smaller operators very volatile.

The Internet has opened the door to communications and information sharing in a way that China has never experienced before. Despite government censorship of sensitive topics and the blockage of taboo web sites, computers and cell phones have become a mainline media source for the nation's thought leaders. Blogs are read daily by corporate executives and government officials. The relentlessly growing demand for Internet access bodes well for Chinese web portals like sina.com (SINA) and sohu.com (SOHU).

Computer makers are experiencing growth rates well over 100 percent,[6] with companies like Lenovo (LNVGY) leading the charge. According to the *Xinhua* news agency, China's computer companies raked in profits of more than $3 billion during the first six months of 2007, up 600 percent from the same period the year before. The nation's 100 leading information technology companies sold more than 12 million computers in China over the first half of 2007, with profits for the top 100 companies in the sector rising 112 percent. Some Chinese telecom equipment companies are now targeting the U.S. market, competing directly with Cisco and Nortel.

The Road Ahead

China may have skipped over much of the twentieth-century communications revolution, but it is determined to compete, and perhaps even dominate, the twenty-first century in a truly globalized, information-driven economy. This is an attractive and accessible investment arena with a great deal of room for further growth.

PART

III

UNDERSTANDING CHINA'S FINANCIAL CENTERS

11

Beijing—The Epicenter of a Capitalist Revolution

He who knows when he can fight and when he cannot, will be victorious.

—Sun Tzu

Beijing, the epicenter of China's capitalist revolution, is a city that reminds me a great deal of Washington, D.C. Not that Beijing resembles Washington in its appearance; it doesn't resemble Washington by its urban architecture very much at all. Where Beijing does resemble the U.S. capital a great deal, however, is in the fairly predictable thought processes of its residents.

If you turn on any U.S. Sunday morning talk show, you will probably hear the latest about what is going on inside the Beltway—that is, the topical focus for the next hour of the program will be on the decisions that have been made in the very center of America's capital. After recapping the latest changes in national policy, these shows will typically proceed to debate how the decisions made inside the Beltway will affect the rest of the country and often the entire world.

Beijing, China's capital, works pretty much the same way. Just as in Washington, Beijing also has a beltway (well, okay, Beijing has several beltways, which they call ring roads). In fact, at present,

Beijing has seven ring roads, with more on the drawing board. Perhaps they need more beltways, because unlike Washington, which has a population of fewer than 1 million residents, Beijing has a population of more than 15 million. Given that Beijing's population size is roughly 10 times that of Manhattan, the stories you have heard about serious pollution problems in Beijing are regrettably true. Even to a first-time visitor, however, it is obvious that Beijing is a very prosperous city.

Decisions made in Beijing definitely affect every part of China. More and more, however, they also affect the entire world, both politically and economically. Not that this is a bad thing. I would argue that it is absolutely necessary for China's influence to be recognized, accepted, and respected if we are to maintain a world of peace and prosperity. But let's be honest about it. If we think a bit, we would all have to admit that China's rise to economic world power status makes China's increase in global political influence inevitable. The sooner we accept this reality, and stop attacking this obvious fact about China's emerging supremacy, the more effective we will be in accomplishing our own national and international goals in this new world environment.

What's more, it is undeniable to anyone (excepting, of course, the aforementioned Lou Dobbs and Pat Buchanan) that China's leadership has quickly brought more wealth to more people than ever accomplished before in human history. Frankly, as an unabashed capitalist myself, my hat is off to China on the wealth creation score.

The problem, at times, comes when members of the old style, supposedly wealthy world economies treat China as if it were a second-class citizen among developed nations. Not a savvy strategy toward the same China that already is the largest holder of U.S. debt and that will in a few years have the world's largest economy. As a student of financial history, I recognize it as the same mistake that the European ruling class made with regard to Baron Rothschild following the Napoleonic Wars. The Euro-snobs of that era snubbed the Rothschilds because they thought they were socially inferior, just as many Westerners snub China today. This ethnocentric attitude was and still is not a smart mentality. Many of those Western investors who fail to study the past, unfortunately, tend to get expensive lessons in the future.

The Sites of Beijing

Beijing, in addition to being China's modern political center, is rich in history. Just as in Washington, you will find the legacy of times past, a period of centuries when China was once before the world's largest economy. But unlike Washington, Beijing holds not only some of mankind's most interesting ancient sites; it is also the home to some of the modern world's most modern structures as well.

When you visit Beijing, the capitalist world's new Mecca, here are my suggestions for must-see sites:

The Great Wall: Started in 750 B.C., the Great Wall is one of the Seven Wonders of the World. In Beijing, the Great Wall was built primarily during the Ming Dynasty. If you don't mind crowds, see the Ba Da Ling section, about two hours from the city center by bus. Take the cable car to get to the top, and bring your camera!

The Forbidden City: This UNESCO World Heritage Site is the world's largest palace compound. You could spend an entire week exploring the Forbidden City, which 24 of China's emperors called home. Enter at Wu Men, the Meridian Gate, and hire a guide to get oriented.

Tian'anmen Square: Built in 1417, Tian'anmen is the Gate of Heavenly Peace, and the square around it is the largest central square in the world. Leading to the Forbidden City, the gate now features Chairman Mao's portrait.

Temple of Heaven: Built during the Ming Dynasty, the Temple of Heaven is the largest imperial worship architecture group in the world, and is larger than the Forbidden City. The temples and impressive gardens will be a welcome respite from the bustle of Beijing.

Summer Palace: Situated on the shores of the enchanting Kuming Lake in the suburbs of Beijing, the Summer Palace is serene beauty exemplified. See how the emperor and his family lived outside of Beijing, amid 717 acres of imperial gardens.

Peking Man Site: Located at Zhoukoudian, roughly 30 miles from Beijing, the Site of Peking Man was discovered by Chinese paleoanthropologist Pei Wenzhong in 1929. Peking Man lived in the Beijing area 690,000 years ago, and the fossils found in the cave date back 10,000 years.

Peking (Beijing) Opera: The Peking Opera has delighted audiences around the world for 200 years. Make time to see the acrobatics, dance, and song that is considered opera in China. Performances take place at the Beijing Huguang Hall, a nineteenth-century guildhall, with its own museum dedicated to Chinese opera.

Lama Temple: Once the home of Prince Yin Zhen, this Qing Dynasty temple is now dedicated to Tibetan Buddhism, which is evident by the throngs of Tibetan monks. The buildings and gardens are both ornate and formal. The Lama Temple is truly a magnificent sight to see.

Prince Gong's Mansion: Built in 1777, Prince Gong's Mansion is the largest mansion from the Qing Dynasty. The complex covers nearly 15 acres, which includes a seven-acre garden, three courtyards, a pavilion with more than 40 rooms, and a grand theater house.

Beihai Park: Located behind the Forbidden City, this park has a history going back five dynasties (10,000 years). Within the park is Qionghua Island, the Five-Dragon Pavilion with its floating bridges, and other pavilions, buildings, and a restaurant.

After familiarizing yourself with Beijing's past, and getting its tourist activities out of your system, it would be a good idea to get a picture of Beijing's likely future. To do that, I would suggest you spend some time on Chang'an Street. Chang'an Street is Beijing's premier business and commercial boulevard. It houses not only many of Beijing's central government buildings, it also is the home to some of the most elite boutiques and shopping this side of Beverly Hill's Rodeo Drive.

How, you may ask yourself, does a supposedly poor Third World country sustain luxury shops with names like Cartier, Tiffany, and Ferragamo? The answer is not by catering to wealthy tourists. The answer, much like with the Rothschilds of the nineteenth century, is that the supposedly poor residents of China are often more wealthy than many of us in the United States.

Of course the most spectacular sights of twenty-first-century Beijing are the new Olympic venues, China's showcase to the world, demonstrating the nation's new status as a modern superpower. China has always placed a high priority on training its athletes and winning gold medals, and the new Olympic venues are designed to be prizewinners in their own right. Long after the games are over, most Olympic cities proudly display their most memorable venues. Beijing's innovative "bird's nest stadium" stands proudly among them.

Olympic venues are only one element of Beijing's architectural declaration that it has arrived on the world stage in a very big way. Stand aside, Chicago. Forget Dubai. Beijing wants to be the world's next great architectural city. To see an example, gaze at the spectacular titanium and glass bubble that appears to be floating in a lake adjacent to the Great Hall of the People. Although it seems light enough to be blown downstream, this bubble houses the massive National Center for the Performing Arts, a showpiece structure that contains an elegant, silk-wallpapered theater, a luxurious opera house, and a stunning concert hall that features China's biggest pipe organ. With soaring public spaces and seating for more than 5,000, the center's *bubble on a pond* concept is a remarkable contrast to the ponderous Stalinist architecture that used to be the norm for major public buildings in the communist world.

One more architectural standout cements Beijing's status as a laboratory for the boisterous and avant-garde in public architecture. The China Central Television tower is a $600 million project that must be seen to be believed. To say that it will become one of the largest buildings in the world in terms of floor space, or that as the home of Beijing's government broadcaster CCTV it will be the world's largest corporate headquarters, falls far short of explaining this building's impact and ambition. With two sloping towers for legs, the CCTV building is topped by a massive angular complex that hangs 525 feet above the ground. Some say the mirrored building looks like it will fall down and others say it is a wild extravagance that sends the wrong message to a country that needs to focus on conserving resources. But Beijing is sending a message to the world, and that message is all about newfound wealth and power.

Big Government

Beijing is also competing with other cities in China for financial influence, housing the headquarters of 10 of China's top 20 domestic commercial banks. Not surprisingly, three large state-owned banks and two state-controlled insurance companies are officially based in the nation's capital, where they used to take orders only from their political masters. As discussed in Chapter 9 (Banking and Finance), most of the old policy banks now have shareholders as well as the government to answer to.

It would be a mistake to assume that China's capitalist revolution has eliminated the role of big government in the affairs of business and the economy. Just as it does in the United States, the central government does its best to manage the macroeconomy, attempting to create as many jobs as possible without creating runaway inflation. Unlike the U.S. system, the Chinese government continues to be a major player in the world of business and it remains a majority shareholder in hundreds of national corporations, referred to previously as state-owned enterprises (SOEs).

Because the nation is still in transition from the Maoist days of central planning, the central government controls the world of business on many levels. National electricity-generating corporations, for example, are subject to national standards and regulations as they might also be in the United States. But Beijing also controls what rates consumers will pay for electricity. Coal-fired generating stations can be temporarily shut down by government decree to reduce air pollution and to improve China's image around the globe during the Olympic Games. Negotiations with France, Japan, Russia, the United States, and Canada over the future construction of nuclear power stations are a matter of international diplomacy, overseen by the highest levels of government in Beijing, not by independent electricity companies. By the same token, China's publicly traded oil and petrochemical corporations are subject to the political intrigues of Beijing. Pump prices of gasoline and other refined petrochemicals are government controlled and some refiners have been forced to operate at a loss to pacify consumers. On the other hand, Beijing's profit-conscious bureaucrats have bailed out energy companies and banks with multibillion-dollar subsidies.

Beijing's mandarins can take a hand in almost any aspect of the business world if the national interest is deemed to be at stake. That's especially true of giant SOEs, but even smaller enterprises are affected by policy decisions made in the capital. More than in any other capitalist country, investors need to pay attention to the policies and trends of the central government because of Beijing's disproportionate clout in the business world. China may have left its communist history in the past, but it will be a very long time before Beijing relaxes its authoritarian ways. In China's capital, managing business is an integral part of managing the country.

CHAPTER 12

Shenzhen—China's Test City

Life's tragedy is that we get too old too soon and wise too late.
—Benjamin Franklin

More than 25 years after Deng Xiapong gave Shenzhen permission to experiment with capitalism, the city has probably become the biggest and most economically successful city that most Western investors have ever known. The bustling metropolis of Shenzhen is the economic heart of the Guandong special economic zone (SEZ), the first of the regions set aside by Deng Xiaoping to unleash the capitalist experiment in communist China. Since its inception, four more SEZs have been created in China, following the Shenzhen model.

By any measure, Shenzhen has been a stunning example of the power and success of free market capitalism, thriving even in the embrace of a once oppressive communist behemoth. Deng Xiaoping gave Shenzhen preferential treatment and incentives, including offers of cheap land and tax holidays in order to entice economic growth and foster prosperity. In doing so, he sought to draw upon the capital and the entrepreneurial energies of Shenzhen's nearby, spectacularly successful southern neighbor, Hong Kong. Surprisingly, this economical-entrepreneurial marriage worked better than anyone had imagined possible.

The Evolution of Shenzhen

Not so long ago, Shenzhen was a small fishing village that offered little promise of economic prosperity. Intuitively, the government used its natural resources and geographic location to transform it into a booming capitalist epicenter. Built near the mouth of the Pearl River delta, Shenzhen established a number of deepwater harbors and container terminals that have become an essential outlet for the city's ever-expanding manufacturing base. As a result, Shenzhen has become the fourth-busiest port in the world and is the second-busiest port in China, after Shanghai.

Shenzhen was also intended to develop a manufacturing base much like that of Hong Kong. In fact, the city drew away most of Hong Kong's manufacturers and spawned many more factories in the process, thanks to the cheap labor that the city drew from the Chinese hinterlands. The city has spawned some of China's better-known high-tech industries, including Huawei and ZTE Corporation, which are vying to become leading suppliers of telecommunications equipment on a global scale.

The biggest manufacturing operation in Shenzhen and in most of China is Foxconn, which operates a factory that covers more than a square mile of land. Foxconn, also known as Hon Hai Precision Industry Company, is a Taiwanese high-tech firm that does most of its manufacturing in China. The company's Shenzhen facility employs an astonishing 270,000 people, many of whom live in corporate dormitories and dine in company cafeterias. Although you may have never heard of the company before, everyone has heard of its products. The Foxconn plant produces the iPod and the iPhone for Apple, Intel-branded motherboards, computer parts for Dell and Hewlett-Packard, gaming systems for Sony and Nintendo, and cell phones for Motorola.

Unlike surrounding Chinese cities, Shenzhen has escaped the worst of the choking pollution that has come to characterize so much of China's economic miracle. Shenzhen does have an unusually fresh and modern look among China's rapidly industrializing urban environments because it is almost entirely a newly-built city. Along prestigious thoroughfares like Shen Nan Road, glass and steel high-rises stretch more than 70 stories into the air, each structure seeming to look even newer and more modern than the last. Although the city's government likes to portray Shenzhen as something of a garden spot, it does have some environmental hazards. The city's lushly landscaped boulevards are overcrowded with BMWs, Mercedes-Benzes, and Lexus sedans as well as the usual swarm of less expensive Chinese and foreign brand cars. Attempting to cross the street on foot or riding a bicycle is most definitely a threat to life and limb.

Even by Western standards, the sprawl of modern office towers and luxury apartments throughout Shenzhen is breathtaking. As the nation's fastest-growing city over the span of more than two decades, the Chinese have developed a slogan for Shenzhen's ever-changing urban face, "One new high rise every day, and one new boulevard every three days." That hardly seems like an exaggeration when surveying the city's forest of office towers from the heights of Shun Hing Square, a gleaming green glass high-rise, which currently holds pride of place as the city's tallest building. Even the most jaded visitors from New York or Las Vegas would be impressed with almost everything except the city's endless traffic jams.

The Shenzhen Stock Exchange

Another impressive economic feature of the city is the Shenzhen Stock Exchange, but not for its physical appearance. Located in a relatively modest green glass tower, the Shenzhen exchange is almost silent and not at all crowded. It is an entirely electronic stock exchange, modeled after the NASDAQ. The Shenzhen Stock Exchange (SZSE) is intended to provide capital for relatively new high-tech enterprises with much lower values than stocks traded in Shanghai. The exchange says it has 635 listed companies, 35 million registered investors, and 177 exchange members. Since its creation in 1990, the SZSE has generated a market capitalization of approximately $690 billion, a fact brought to life in Figure 12.1. On a daily basis, around 600,000 deals, valued at approximately $807 million, trade on the SZSE.[1] Frankly, these statistics may seem lower than an investor guru would expect and they may already be out of date, considering the spectacular rise in share values over the past two years.

Even exchange officials privately admit that they are dealing with a very hot market and that some stocks may be overvalued. Exchange executives are trying to limit excessive volatility by capping trading in a stock if its price moves up or down more than 10 percent in a single day. Companies that trade at the upper limit

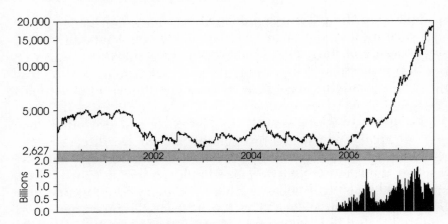

Figure 12.1 Shenzhen Exchange Example
Source: Reproduced with permission of Yahoo! Inc. YAHOO! and the YAHOO! logo are trademarks of Yahoo! Inc. (http://finance.yahoo.com/).

for three days in a row are asked to disclose any known reasons for the volatility of their stock. Exchange officials say that revenues are rising rapidly for SZSE stocks, but valuations are too high for their liking with an average P/E ratio of 40. They are hoping for the creation of a derivatives market by the China Securities Regulatory Commission (CSRC) to help moderate the upward pressure on stock prices.

The Shenzhen market has also developed what it calls an SME board, a separate exchange that trades in small and medium-size enterprises. Most of the action in Shenzhen is off-limits to foreigners unless they are Qualified Foreign Institutional Investors (QFIIs). Foreigners who make the grade may be restricted to trade in B shares, shares which are denominated in Hong Kong dollars. Investor gurus, please take note: This market trades for only four hours a day, from 9:30 to 11:30 A.M. and from 1:00 to 3:00 P.M. local time.

The Next World Capital Alliance

As a city, Shenzhen has grown so rapidly and covered so much territory that it has virtually merged with its predecessor and mentor, Hong Kong. Shenzhen certainly has a larger population than Hong Kong, with an official tally of approximately 8.5 million, compared to Hong Kong's population of slightly less than 7 million. Informal estimates of Shenzen's population run as high as 12 million because of the influx of undocumented migrant workers from other provinces.

Chinese citizens who travel between Shenzhen and Hong Kong must go through customs and immigration checkpoints before they enter either city. Hong Kong says it is considering a plan that could allow Shenzhen's registered residents to enter Hong Kong freely. If approved, the measure would be the first step toward creating a unified Hong Kong–Shenzhen metropolis.

Together, Hong Kong and Shenzhen have ambitions to become a world financial capital, on a par with New York, London, and Tokyo. Physical links between the two cities are increasing daily, but it remains to be seen whether Beijing will entertain the creation of a new supercity on China's southern coast.

CHAPTER 13

Shanghai—China's Own Manhattan

A bank book makes good reading—better than some novels.
—Harry Lauder

Shanghai is the kind of city that deserves—and has—its own book. A brief chapter can hardly do justice to China's biggest and most complex metropolis.

Although other Chinese cities are economically prosperous, Shanghai is considered by many to be China's finance and banking capital. The city now ranks as number three among world financial centers, behind only New York and London. With its soaring skyline, it now has more skyscrapers than New York and it is home to more than 500 multinational corporations. Although major economic reforms didn't get under way in Shanghai until 1992, which is more than a decade later than in the special economic zone of Shenzhen, Shanghai has quickly reclaimed its place as the economic hub of China.

Unlike Shenzhen, its boomtown sister city to the South, Shanghai is a city with a history going back 700 years. From its origins as a trading center at the mouth of the Yangtze River, Shanghai has grown to become the world's busiest port, handling approximately 450 million tons of cargo every year. The bulk of China's industrial and manufacturing output is sent out to the world from Shanghai's massive container terminal.

Many Westerners will have seen photographs of the new Shanghai skyline, with its iconic Oriental Pearl TV Tower dominating the city. The city's office buildings, with their eye-catching, and futuristic appearance and high-powered lighting, loom over the city, metaphorically pronouncing their dominance as an economic power. As in Manhattan, height and architecture speak volumes about a company's relative financial importance in China's new capitalist economy.

The famous view of the Pudong financial center's skyscrapers and the Oriental Pearl TV Tower across the Huangpu River captures only a fragment of Shanghai's scale and its momentum. Along the river, huge illuminated billboards glide past throngs of shoppers, advertising the city's wealth of consumer goods. (A fast-growing Chinese advertising pioneer, Focus Media (FMCN), runs the glaring river billboards and thousands of illuminated electronic posters in posh high-rise elevators.)

This city of 21 million people is so large that it has earned official status as a full-fledged province in the structure of the Chinese government. It has a public transportation system approximately the size of London's network, with almost 1,000 bus lines.

The Face of New Money

Arriving at one of the city's two main airports and traveling to the heart of the business district provides a remarkable prism from which to view the new Shanghai and the new China. Offshore, a few miles from the Pudong airport, lines of tankers steam into the port, providing imported oil, the lifeblood of every Chinese city. Pudong Airport, with its sweeping roofs and immensely long terminals, speaks volumes about the scale and ultramodern ambitions of the city itself. The airport is expected to become the largest in the world by 2015 with three vast terminals and five runways handling a staggering 100 million passengers a year. Passengers who wish to skip past Shanghai traffic can be whisked silently to the city by an advanced, elevated Maglev train.

The wealth of the Shanghai region is apparent not only in the glittering towers of the city's many business districts or its spotless transportation facilities. On the suburban roads surrounding the city, new apartment complexes rise skyward, some of them reaching unprecedented levels of garishness. The richest of these buildings mix nineteenth century Parisian profiles with elaborate Greco-Roman decoration. Yet another example of how money talks in Shanghai, sometimes very, very loudly.

The old and the new rub shoulders in Shanghai unlike any of the freshly minted special economic zones. Along the broad, new highways and boulevards leading into Shanghai, major intersections carry workers to vast factories with familiar multinational names like General Motors, Toyota, and ABB (the giant Swiss engineering, electric power, and automation conglomerate). Shanghai's old and historic financial district, the Bund, is filled with luxury shops, restaurants, and glittering department stores. But among those lavish shops and streets, you can also find an entire mall devoted to fake goods: inexpensive, counterfeit copies of Western brand name items.

The city also faces severe challenges from pollution, overcrowding, and traffic and it is creating satellite cities to absorb its burgeoning population. Competing urban centers, including Beijing and Hong Kong, continue to fight for a share of Shanghai's riches. Still, one can't help but admire and believe in a city that rose from infamy and stagnation to become one of the world's financial capitals in 15 short years. It's the kind of economic miracle that only the United States used to be capable of.

Shanghai's Economic Engine

Shanghai may have been a late starter in the Chinese manufacturing boom, but it has most certainly caught up. The gross domestic product of the Shanghai region is estimated at a staggering $450 billion, half the size of the entire economy of India.[1] The city proper has a GDP of $134 billion. The BBC estimates that the Shanghai region, with its two adjoining provinces, accounts for 30 percent of China's foreign exports and 20 percent of the nation's manufacturing.

The financial services industry accounts for 7.8 percent of Shanghai's economy.[2] Ninety-eight foreign banks are vying for office space and for customers in the new Shanghai. This is an astonishing turnaround for a city that was closed to foreign financiers by Chairman Mao. During Mao's communist revolution, overseas banks fled to Hong Kong to enjoy capitalism's freedoms. When China began to reopen its doors to capitalism, Shanghai became the first Chinese city to open itself to foreign financial institutions. Soon after, foreign banks began to swarm into the Pudong district to stake out their turf. Logos of the world's financial giants, including Citigroup, now struggle vainly for visibility among Shanghai's tallest towers, which are dominated by the likes of the Bank of China and China Life.

A rivalry for financial dominance has developed between Hong Kong and Shanghai and it continues to this day. Hong Kong's bankers and financiers are ever the salesmen, touting their easy access to the Chinese mainland. But Shanghai barely has to struggle to compete because foreign and Chinese banks now flock to this city, which is the new center of China's financial action.

The Chinese government has made a change from its early sense of ambivalence toward domestic stock markets. In the 1990s, the nation's biggest and most important corporations were listed in other parts of the world before investors in Shanghai and Shenzhen could take a stake in them. The early days of China's internal stock markets had been marred by spectacular failures, insider trading, and other forms of corruption. The abuses of the system at times were so egregious that major riots broke out over secret "internal distribution" of share offerings by the state-controlled Peoples Bank of China (PBOC).[3] It turned out that the PBOC was acting as a player in the markets rather than a regulator, forcing Beijing to create the China Securities Regulatory Commission (CSRC).

Corruption was not eliminated quickly or easily in Shanghai or Shenzhen by the fledgling, inexperienced CSRC. Figure 13.1 depicts the Shanghai Composite Index. While looking at the figure, you will see a multiyear slump, caused by widespread investor discouragement with stock market regulation.

The Chinese government is now funneling major IPOs into the Shanghai stock exchange, making some of China's state-owned corporations among the biggest in the world, measured by market capitalization (among them are the Industrial and Commercial Bank of China, China Life, and PetroChina). The government has two good reasons for funneling new IPOs into the giant Shanghai exchange. First, Beijing's mandarins hope to spread out the funds of inexperienced investors who have bid up the values of smaller companies to unrealistic levels. Second, the government is hoping that an increasing flow of investment money into the stock market

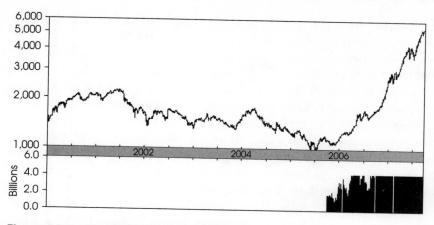

Figure 13.1 Shanghai Composite Index
Source: Reproduced with permission of Yahoo! Inc. YAHOO! and the YAHOO! logo are
trademarks of Yahoo! Inc. (http://finance.yahoo.com/).

may help soak up excess liquidity, which is driving up real estate
prices to levels that may be unsustainable.

Many old brokerages went bankrupt or faced prosecution during Shanghai's protracted market slump. New firms are thriving but
there is still something of a Wild West atmosphere to investing in
Shanghai. Unless you invest solely online, you may find yourself in a
back alley, looking for a brokerage that looks more like the betting
window at a dog track than an oak-paneled boardroom. The scene
at such a brokerage brings home the contrast between the old and
the new Shanghai.

The Old and the New

Miles from Pudong's gleaming towers, dingy rooms are filled with
China's retail investors, shouting and playing cards as they glance at
monitors flashing the latest changes in stock prices. There is no CNBC
or Fox Financial Channel to interpret the market's fluctuations,
just the apparent superstitions of gray-haired women and men who
gamble on a stock market that, like Shenzhen's market, may be in a
bubble. It currently has no derivatives or short-selling mechanisms
that would create an incentive to drive prices down. (The authorities say various forms of derivatives are in the works and that Chinese
investors may also be allowed to bet on *H* shares in Hong Kong.)

But, before we judge Chinese investors too harshly, take a closer look at the antique computer monitors that fill Shanghai's brokerage offices. Along with computer-generated charts, we see Bollinger Bands, MACD indicators, and classic "candlesticks"—which are the tools of technical analysts. Perhaps Shanghai's retail investors are more sophisticated than the government credits them with being.

Remarkably, the future Shanghai may be even more remarkable than today's instant city. Visit the Shanghai Urban Planning Exhibition Hall near People's Square and you will see a model of the city as it is expected to look in 2020. The scale of architecture on display is overwhelming. The exhibit is big enough to cover a volleyball court. Shanghai's economy is expected by 2020 to have grown fivefold, making it the richest economic region in the world.

CHAPTER 14

Taiwan—The Breakaway Prodigy

It is better to have a permanent income than to be fascinating.
—Oscar Wilde

Known by many names, the island of Taiwan has been another outstanding performer among the Greater China economies and the so-called Asian Tiger economies. At once a center of international tension and political intrigue, Taiwan and its capital city of Taipei have defied predictions that the island nation would be invaded and swallowed by mainland China. After breaking away from the mainland's political influence during Mao Zedong's revolution, Taiwan managed to transform itself from an underdeveloped, agricultural island with few natural resources into an economic powerhouse that has become a leading producer of high technology goods and manufacturing centers in the world.

Building the Beautiful Island

Originally called Formosa or *beautiful island* by Portuguese explorers in the 1600s, Taiwan adopted the controversial name *Republic of China* after breaking away from the government of mainland China in the wake of Chairman Mao's communist revolution in 1949. Two million nationalists fled to the island with a substantial portion of China's currency reserves, and adopted a constitution that claimed sovereignty over all of China. But while Chairman Mao was busy spreading communist revolution among mainland Chinese, the Taiwanese were busy making money by becoming one of the world's great high-tech manufacturing centers.

During the 1960s, foreign investment in Taiwan helped introduce modern, labor-intensive technology to the island. With U.S. assistance, Taiwan became a major exporter of labor-intensive products, such as shoes and textile-based goods. Products were usually stamped *Made in China* to the dismay of the mainland government, which claimed to be the one true China and claimed sovereignty over the island of Taiwan.

As the island built its economic engine, the total value of international trade with Taiwan increased more than fivefold in the 1960s. While the mainland struggled through the communist revolution under Chairman Mao, Taiwanese trade grew nearly tenfold in the 1970s, and doubled again in the 1980s. The 1990s saw a more modest level of trade growth because of the Asian financial crisis.

During the 1980s, Taiwan's focus shifted increasingly toward sophisticated, capital-intensive and technology-intensive products for export. The nation also focused on developing the service sector. The electronics industry is now Taiwan's most important industrial export sector and is the largest recipient of U.S. investment. During the 1980s and 1990s, Taiwan became the world's largest supplier of computer monitors. It currently remains a leading personal computer manufacturer. Taiwan Semiconductor Manufacturing (TSM) is one of the world's largest suppliers of silicon chip products. Many other Taiwanese companies have followed in TSM's footsteps, including the highly automated textile production industry, which continues to be an important industrial export sector.

The success of Taiwan's trading practices continues today. The United States is Taiwan's second-largest trading partner, receiving 20 percent of Taiwan's exports and supplying 16 percent of its imports. Taiwan is the United States's eighth-largest trading partner. Taiwan's two-way trade with the United States exceeds $45 billion.

Real growth in Taiwanese GDP has averaged about 8 percent during the past three decades. Exports have grown even faster and have provided the primary engine for industrialization. Inflation and unemployment are low, the trade surplus is substantial, and Taiwan's foreign reserves are among the world's largest pools of capital, exceeding $500 billion. Also, the appreciation of the New

Taiwan dollar (NT), rising labor costs, and increasing environmental consciousness in Taiwan has caused many labor-intensive industries, such as shoe manufacturing, to move to mainland China and less developed regions of Southeast Asia.

It remains to be seen how much future economic development will occur on the island of Taiwan itself. Taiwan has now become a major investor in the People's Republic of China (PRC), Thailand, Indonesia, the Philippines, Malaysia, and Vietnam.

The Love-Hate Relationship

Taiwan's economic success has been remarkable considering the island nation's status as a political outsider on the world stage. Because of mainland China's enormous political clout and its growing economic muscle, most trading nations have been extremely reluctant to reestablish diplomatic relations with the renegade island. Few countries dare to give offense to the PRC, which is expected to become the world's largest economy.

Money has a way, though, of trumping politics. The lack of formal diplomatic relations with all but a few of its trading partners appears not to have seriously hindered Taiwan's continuously expanding commerce. Taiwan maintains trade offices in more than 60 countries with which it does not have official diplomatic relations. In addition to the World Trade Organization (WTO), Taiwan is a member of the Asia Development Bank under the name *Taipei, China* and the Asia-Pacific Economic Cooperation (APEC) forum under yet another name: *Chinese Taipei*.

Taiwan's stock exchange has been affected by that nation's love-hate relationship with mainland China. Tension between the two countries and occasional military threats disrupt business and consumer confidence. At the same time, increasing amounts of Taiwanese investment capital is sent across the straits to the mainland as investors try to take advantage of the mainland's exceptionally cheap labor and ongoing economic growth.

Despite China's deep hostility to the Taiwanese government and all forms of Taiwanese nationalism, the two entities are best of enemies. China has overtaken the United States to become Taiwan's largest export market and its second-largest source of imports after Japan. China is also the island's number one destination for foreign direct investment.

China says trade with Taiwan rose to a record level of $108.7 billion in 2006, an increase of 18 percent from the year before. Tourism between the mainland and the island of Taiwan is also flourishing.[1] Despite the public hostility between the two entities, a remarkable four million Taiwanese visited the mainland in 2006, while 200,000 people from the Chinese mainland made the trip to Taiwan.

Taiwan is investing billions in mainland China's development. The Chinese Ministry of Commerce says it approved more than $11 billion worth of Taiwanese projects in 2006.[2]

The Taiwanese stock market recovered from the shock of the Asian economic crisis of 1997–1998. The Taiex Index was also badly shaken by the tech wreck that decimated the NASDAQ in 2001–2002. During 2007, the index rebounded to highs of almost 90,000. Figure 14.1 illustrates the rise and fall of the Taiex over several years.

Despite ongoing nervousness about the tension between Taiwan and the PRC, the island nation's economy remains strong and stable. Its Gross Domestic Product measured by PPP is estimated at $681 billion and continues to grow at approximately 4.7 percent per year.[3]

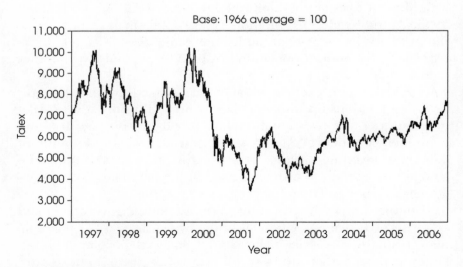

Figure 14.1   Taiex Index
Source: Reproduced with permission of Yahoo! Inc. YAHOO! and the YAHOO! logo are trademarks of Yahoo! Inc. (http://finance.yahoo.com/).

A Foggy Future?

Although Taiwan has experienced a great deal of economic prosperity, the island nation now faces many of the same economic issues as other developed Asian economies. With the prospect of continued relocation of labor-intensive industries to countries with cheaper work forces, Taiwan's future development will have to rely on further transformation to an increasingly high technology and service-oriented economy. Moreover, textile production is declining in importance for Taiwan as the island loses its competitive advantage to cheap-labor economies.

Overshadowing all other considerations is the extreme hostility Taiwan faces from the People's Republic of China. Beijing feels no compunction about threatening war if Taiwan openly declares its independence. Both sides are heavily armed and the quantity and sophistication of China's armaments is growing exponentially. Although an outbreak of hostilities may seem unlikely from distant shores, it is a real danger and it makes stock markets nervous.

I believe, personally, that both sides will back away from the brink and that recognition of the advantages of trade and cooperation will knit Taiwan and the People's Republic into a close relationship, a relationship that makes much more economic sense than making or even threatening war. The rise and fall of hostility between the two sides will nevertheless continue to add an element of volatility to Taiwanese stocks and ADRs because of the dire economic consequences that would follow an outbreak of war.

CHAPTER

15

Hong Kong—China's
Modern Frontier

He who will not economize will have to agonize.
—Confucius

More than 10 years after its return to China, Hong Kong
retains its reputation as the world's freest economy. The city has
been awarded that honor for 13 consecutive years, a period span-
ning its existence as a British colony and as a part of China, by both
the Heritage Foundation and the *Wall Street Journal*.

Building an Economic Cornerstone

The Hong Kong economy enjoyed decades of spectacular growth
under a century and a half of British rule, evolving from a trading
hub to an inexpensive manufacturing center to becoming the banking and financial services nexus for Southeast Asia. With an aggressive and well-educated workforce, Hong Kong manages to stay on
top economically. Even setbacks seem to be overcome with remarkable speed by Hong Kong's extraordinary work ethic.

Hong Kong has endured and recovered from repeated economic
tremors in recent years. First, there was the Asian currency crisis of
the late 1990s, which caused a 5.3 percent decline in the economy
in 1998. Then the high-tech stock bubble burst on Wall Street and

sent shock waves around the world, causing some reverberations in Hong Kong. The worldwide scare over the Severe Acute Respiratory Syndrome (SARS) virus and the HN51 bird flu virus struck at Hong Kong's reputation for safety. In particular, the SARS health scare was especially hard on the economy as tourists and business travelers canceled their plans to visit the "special administrative region," causing a 2.3 percent economic decline.

Overshadowing all of the other economic tremors was the political earthquake caused by the handover of Hong Kong from British to Chinese rule on June 30, 1997. Fortunately, under the terms of the sovereignty deal, the People's Republic of China (PRC) agreed to grant Hong Kong special status during the takeover period, which has yielded economic benefits for both sides.

For the time being, Hong Kong is governed as a special administrative region (SAR), still operating under the British-legislated Basic Law of Hong Kong. Under the terms of the Sino-British Joint Declaration, the PRC has promised that Hong Kong will have a relatively high degree of autonomy until at least 2047, which is 50 years after the transfer of sovereignty. Under this unique *One Country, Two Systems* policy, Hong Kong retains its own legal system, currency, customs policy, cultural delegation, international sport teams, and immigration laws, while the PRC represents Hong Kong diplomatically and militarily.

By any measure, the handover was an extraordinarily pragmatic arrangement agreed to by the PRC. The Hong Kong economy has now returned to full health, with the real GDP rising dramatically for more than two years. GDP rose by 8.6 percent during 2004, by 7.3 percent in 2005, and by a remarkable rate of 6.6 percent during 2006.

The Transformation of an Economy

Over the years, Hong Kong's economy has transitioned from a labor-intensive manufacturing base to an overwhelming concentration on service industries. The four economic pillars of Hong Kong are made up of crucial service sectors that include trade and logistics, which constitutes 27.6 percent of GDP; financial services, 12.2 percent; tourism, 2.9 percent; and professional services and other producer services, 10.5 percent. Taking all service sectors into account, they make up 90 percent of the economy.

Hong Kong is now number one in Asia as measured by personal wealth and per capita production. Put in perspective, Hong Kong's economic strength overwhelms its closest Chinese rival, Shanghai, which, in a recent comparison, had a per capita GDP of $5,620. Hong Kong produced an exceptional GDP of $37,400, more than the per capita GDP of some developed Western economies.

Hong Kong's external sector, including the high value tourism industry, also showed robust growth in 2005. In 2005, a total of 23.4 million visitors, or 3.4 times the size of the local population, came to Hong Kong, representing a 7.1 percent increase from 2004. From January through August of 2006, tourist arrivals rose by 10.4 percent year on year. Tourists from the Chinese mainland accounted for more than half of the total.

Trade with China is an increasingly important engine in Hong Kong's robust growth. Despite its small geographical size, Hong Kong is the world's eleventh-largest trading economy.

Hong Kong's major export trade market is the Chinese mainland, which received 47 percent of Hong Kong's total exports during the first eight months of 2006. During that period, the city's exports to the Chinese mainland surged by 13.7 percent. Hong Kong's trade performance is partly fueled by labor-intensive outsourcing to Guangdong, where the majority of Hong Kong companies have extended their manufacturing base.

Hong Kong is also the largest source of overseas direct investment in the Chinese mainland. By the end of 2005, the largest portion of all the overseas-funded projects registered in mainland China were tied to Hong Kong interests. Capital inflow from Hong Kong amounted to $259.5 billion, accounting for 41.7 percent of the national total.

By the same token, the Chinese mainland is one of the leading investors in Hong Kong. According to one analysis, the mainland's cumulative direct investment in Hong Kong was $130.8 billion or 29 percent of Hong Kong's total stock of inward direct investment at the end of 2004. It is estimated that there are over 2,000 mainland-backed enterprises registered in Hong Kong, with total assets exceeding $220 billion.

Hong Kong functions as an international banking hub for China, Asia, and the world. There are 16 Chinese banks and 7 representative offices operating in Hong Kong. The Bank of China has now become the second-largest banking group in Hong Kong, dwarfed only by the international giant HSBC. China's other big lenders, including Industrial and Commercial Bank of China, Agricultural Bank of China, and China Construction Bank, have also opened branch operations in Hong Kong.

The Basis of the Boom

As shown in Figure 15.1, Hong Kong's stock market is the second largest in Asia and the seventh largest in the world, when measured by market capitalization.

Market performance as measured by the Hang Seng Index continues to be impressive. It has set new record highs, as increasing numbers of mainland firms seek to be listed on the Hong Kong Exchange. As mentioned earlier, the listing of the Industrial and Commercial Bank set a record as the world's largest IPO.

Many companies operating in China are managed from headquarters in Hong Kong. Mainland Chinese firms, especially those with state ownership are traded on the Hong Kong market as *H Shares*.

Hong Kong is a popular venue for regional headquarters or branch offices for multinational companies that manage their businesses in the Asia Pacific region. Based on a government survey, a total of 3,845 overseas companies had regional operations in Hong Kong on June 1, 2006. This is a 20 percent increase from three years earlier. The United States has the largest total number of regional

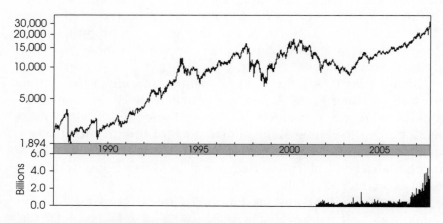

Figure 15.1   Hong Kong Hang Seng Index
Source: Reproduced with permission of Yahoo! Inc. YAHOO! and the YAHOO! logo are trademarks of Yahoo! Inc. (http://finance.yahoo.com/).

headquarters and offices in Hong Kong, with 889 companies, followed by Japan (731), the United Kingdom (337), and the Chinese mainland (268). The trend is on the upswing. The number of regional headquarters and offices whose parent companies were from the United States, Japan, and the United Kingdom, for example, all increased by 20 percent from June 2003 to June 2006. Those from the Chinese mainland increased 33 percent in those three short years.

Hong Kong has weathered the worst economic storms of the Asia Pacific region and still comes out on top. With the continuing emergence of China, Hong Kong is positioned to serve both the Chinese economic colossus and to be a bridge between China and the rest of Asia and the industrialized Western world.

The Secret of the Gateway

Hong Kong residents are fond of saying they have only their people, their intelligence, and their knowledge to make the economy run. With no natural resources to speak of, aside from a world-class harbor, Hong Kong depends on its highly competitive people to retain its status as the indispensable economic gateway between China and the rest of the world.

PART IV

BUILDING A CHINA STOCK GURU PORTFOLIO

CHAPTER 16

Buying China Without Leaving Home

Life is really simple, but we insist on making it complicated.
—Confucius

Every fall, I provide an opportunity for a select group of my *China Stock Digest* newsletter subscribers to travel with me deep inside China to see with their own eyes the incredible economic progress China is making. These trips normally fill quickly after they are announced on my *China Stock Digest* web site, as the number of available spaces are limited, and my primary role in life is that of professional investor, not a tour guide.

If you ever are lucky enough to have the chance to come see China with me, you will be in for a real eye-opener. I have built, over the years, solid relationships with senior executives, university researchers, and government officials all over China. This provides me access to one of the most important resources for successful investing: reliable information. I have often learned about new policies and economic opportunities long before they become public knowledge in the West.

If you are interested in traveling to China, please visit my web site at chinastockdigest.com.

Do I Need to Travel to China to Invest?

One of the first questions I am typically asked by new China investors is whether it is necessary to travel to China to purchase Chinese
stocks. The answer is a resounding *No!* China investments can be
easily made right at home in the United States or London, without
ever traveling to China.

There are five basic ways investors can make stock investments
in China:

1. U.S. American Depositary Receipts
2. U.S. mutual funds that invest in China
3. Exchange-traded funds (ETFs) and index funds
4. Chinese companies that trade only in China or Hong Kong
5. U.S. stocks for companies that do significant business in China

Each of these investment approaches has unique advantages
and risks. Before getting into the specific pros and cons of these
approaches, it's important to discuss the nature of the stock markets inside China and the shares they trade.

Chinese stock markets are composed of four unique stock
exchanges. They are the Hong Kong, Shanghai, Shenzhen, and Taipei
markets. These exchanges run under three different market systems.

Hong Kong's stock exchange operates similarly to the London
Stock Exchange. By contrast, the Taipei Stock Exchange is run
according to Taiwanese rules, which are also similar, but not identi-
cal, to the regulations in London and New York. Therefore, one of
the issues investors have to consider with regard to risk is that Hong
Kong and Taipei have a history of financial regulations and legal
systems that are fairly well established and reliable.

The stock exchanges in Shanghai and Shenzhen are run by the
People's Republic of China (PRC). These Chinese exchanges are
operating in a country that has explosive economic growth, but has
yet to have its regulatory infrastructure keep up with it. Although
this is generally true in any emerging market, it creates an added
level of risk in the PRC.

Specifically, the issues of intellectual property protection, financial disclosure, corporate governance, and the amount of information
that gets released to a potential investor all create a higher level of
risk dealing in the Chinese internal markets than you would have in a
more transparent or regulated markets such as those in New York and

London. That's why we place a premium on research and information at my investment research company and in my *China Stock Digest*.

Also, the Chinese market system is still evolving and emerging from a complex financial and political history. There is a confusing variety of shares to be understood. There are *A, B,* and *C* shares traded on the Shanghai and Shenzhen exchanges, while there are *H, N,* and *L* shares traded in New York, Hong Kong, and London.

From one guru to another, I recommend that you avoid most of these shares. Nevertheless, here's a brief primer so you won't be confused by terminology when an alphabet soup of share offerings confronts you:

- *A Shares* are usually held only by Chinese residents and are denominated in yuan (also known as *renminbi*), the local currency of the People's Republic of China. As of 2003, qualified foreign institutional investors (QFIIs) were authorized to trade in *A* shares in Shanghai and Shenzhen. QFIIs must have at least $10 billion in assets under management.
- *B Shares* are designated for foreign investors and are denominated in foreign currencies on the Shanghai and Shenzhen exchanges.
- *C Shares* are owned by state-run corporations and are not yet publicly traded.
- *H Shares* are stocks of companies incorporated in China and listed on the Hong Kong Stock Exchange and on foreign exchanges, such as Singapore.
- *N Shares* are stocks of companies incorporated in China and listed on the New York Stock Exchange, sometimes as over-the-counter (OTC) shares.
- *L Shares* are stocks of companies incorporated in China and listed on the London Stock Exchange.
- *Red Chips* are stocks of Chinese companies incorporated outside the People's Republic and listed in Hong Kong. The business of these companies is conducted within China and they are controlled by shareholders on the mainland.
- *American Depositary Receipts (ADRs) and American Depositary Shares (ADSs)*. ADRs and ADSs are traded on the New York Stock Exchange.
- *Global Depositary Receipts (GDRs)*. GDRs are traded largely on the London Stock Exchange.

When investing in China, you want to focus your efforts where you can receive the best possible return with the least amount of risk. Of the five possible ways to invest in China, therefore, we will focus on only three:

1. American Depositary Receipts
2. U.S. mutual funds that invest in China
3. ETFs and index funds

We will not spend our time on the other two options, namely traveling to China to purchase shares with local Chinese brokerage accounts, nor will we focus on investing in U.S. companies that do business in China as a way to play the China market.

Don't Book Your Plane Ticket Yet

There are various reasons why it does not make sense to travel to China to purchase shares. If you were to travel to China and attempt to open a brokerage account, you would face a number of hurdles that make it completely impractical for most investors. First, you would need to speak Chinese, namely either Mandarin or Cantonese. Very few foreign investors can do this. Second, brokerage firms in Hong Kong would refuse to open a trading account for any American investor unless they maintain a permanent address in Hong Kong and can prove legal Hong Kong residency.

Next, there would be no economic advantage to you if you traveled to China to invest. In mainland China, presuming you can speak enough Mandarin to complete a new account form, you would only be allowed to purchase Chinese *B* share stocks. Most of these *B* shares already trade in the United States as ADRs, so what would be the point of going to China to buy them? You would not be allowed to purchase *A* share stocks because they are offered only to Chinese citizens. So, there is no advantage to going through the hassle required to travel to China to invest in stocks you can easily purchase as ADRs in the United States without the additional language barrier and travel costs.

Would You Invest in a U.S. Company in China?

It is also an unwise decision to buy investments in a U.S. company that is doing business in China simply because it has operations there. The reason is that one cannot adequately estimate how much of an impact the U.S. company's operations in China will have on the firm's overall financial results. For example, General Motors has been quite successful to date in its efforts to establish itself in China. But if its operations in China represent only 1 percent of the company's worldwide income, even if it is successful, you won't see a big impact on the company's stock price.

Most of the people who have an interest in China want to see results in their portfolio over a three-year to five-year period, and they don't want to wait 20 years for a behemoth like General Motors or General Electric to get established enough in China to see meaningful results in their financial performance. As such, it is not recommended that investors buy stock in U.S. companies doing business in China solely or primarily because those companies are doing that.

Guru's Focus on Investments That Work

As a result of the problems noted in two of the methods mentioned (that is, traveling to China to open brokerage accounts and buying stocks of Western companies doing business in China), I focus our attention instead on the three methods that are practical for investing in China. In the next few chapters, I discuss how investing in American Depositary Receipts, U.S. mutual funds that invest in China, and ETFs and index funds will help you profit from China's economic boom.

17

Understanding the Safest Way to Invest in Chinese Stocks

Those that won't be counseled can't be helped.
—Benjamin Franklin

W e need to get a clearer picture of the three viable options for investing in China's stock market to profit from her economic boom: American Depositary Receipts, exchange-traded funds (ETFs)—including exchange-traded index funds—and mutual funds that invest in China. In this chapter we learn about the primary characteristics of these three investment options so that investors can see why they are the safest way to invest in Chinese stocks.*

---

*Each of these products is specifically defined by the U.S. Securities and Exchange Commission in their official literature and on their web site, sec.gov. I have attempted to translate the SEC's more technical definitions into a reader-friendly format. In my efforts, I want to note my appreciation to the SEC in making a standard definition available to the public, and acknowledge their contribution to this chapter from their official literature, which has been adapted for our purposes.

American Depositary Receipts

The stocks of most Chinese companies that trade in the U.S. markets are traded as American Depositary Receipts (ADRs), which are issued by U.S. depositary banks. The acronyms *ADR* and *ADS* (American Depositary Shares) are sometimes used interchangeably. An ADR is actually the physically negotiable certificate that evidences ADSs in much the same way a stock certificate evidences shares of stock. An ADS is the security that represents an ownership interest in deposited securities in much the same way a share of stock represents an ownership interest in a corporation. In other words, ADRs are the instruments actually traded in the market.

Each ADR represents one or more shares or a fraction of a share of a foreign stock. If you own an ADR, you have the right to obtain the foreign stock it represents, but U.S. investors usually find it more convenient to own the ADR. The price of an ADR usually corresponds to the price of the foreign stock in its home market, adjusted for the ratio of ADRs to foreign company shares. In the case of the inflated and economically isolated Shanghai and Shenzhen stock markets, the valuation of an ADR will generally be lower (cheaper) than shares of stock traded on the mainland.

Owning ADRs has some advantages compared to owning foreign shares directly. These advantages include:

- When you buy and sell ADRs, you are trading in the U.S. market. Your trade will consequently clear and settle in U.S. dollars.
- The depositary bank will convert any dividends or other cash payments into U.S. dollars before sending them to you.
- The depositary bank may arrange to vote your shares for you as you instruct.

On the other hand, there are some disadvantages to ADRs, including:

- It may take a long time for you to receive information from the company because it must pass through an extra pair of hands. You may receive information about shareholder meetings only a few days before the meeting, well past the time when you could vote your shares.

- Depositary banks charge fees for their services and will deduct these fees from the dividends and other distributions on your shares. The depositary bank also will incur expenses, such as for converting foreign currency into U.S. dollars, and usually will pass those expenses on to you.
- Curious investors can learn more about the origins of ADRs at investorpedia.com.

Exchange-Traded Funds

Another way to invest internationally in the stock market is through exchange-traded funds (ETFs). An exchange-traded fund is a type of investment whose key objective is to achieve the same return as a particular market index. As such, ETFs are also often referred to as index funds. Increasingly popular with investors, ETFs are listed on stock exchanges and, like stocks (and in contrast to mutual funds), trade at known prices throughout the trading day.

Open-ended mutual funds differ substantially from exchange-traded funds in that they can be bought and sold only once a day. Unlike exchange-traded funds, the price at which you buy or sell your open-ended mutual fund is not known at the time you place the transaction, and will not be set until after the market closes on the day of the purchase or sale.

A share in an ETF that tracks an international index gives exposure to the performance of the underlying stock portfolio along with the ability to trade that share like any other security.

Investors who want to sell their ETF shares generally do this by selling the fund in their brokerage account as if it were any other listed stock.

Owning exchange-traded funds has some advantages compared to owning ADRs or mutual funds, including:

- When you buy an ETF, you receive the benefit of diversification among the numerous stocks that make up the index the ETF is attempting to mimic. This reduces the stock-specific risk that can arise from owning ADR shares.
- When you buy an ETF, you do not normally pay significant sales charges, known as loads, which are common to many stock mutual funds.

On the other hand, there are some disadvantages common to ETFs, including:

- ETFs can, at times, have more price volatility than open-ended mutual funds. This is because the ability to trade these funds throughout a market day at fixed prices has sometimes attracted speculators and day traders to this type of investment.
- ETFs can, at times, reduce your portfolio's diversification (compared to some open-ended mutual funds) because they tend to overweight their portfolio among those stocks that have a larger market value (also known as market capitalization).

Mutual Funds

Mutual funds that invest in China are another viable option for investing in China's stock market. A mutual fund is a company that pools money from many investors and places the money in stocks or other securities or assets, or some combination of these investments. The combined holdings the mutual fund owns are known as its portfolio. Each share represents an investor's proportionate ownership of the fund's holdings and the income those holdings generate.

There are different kinds of funds that invest in foreign stocks. Here's how they work:

- *Global funds* invest primarily in foreign companies, but may also invest in U.S. companies.
- *International funds* generally limit their investments to companies outside the United States.
- *Regional* or *country funds* invest principally in companies located in a particular geographical region (such as Asia) or in a single country, such as China. Some funds invest only in emerging markets, while others concentrate on more developed markets.

International investing through mutual funds can reduce some of the risks mentioned earlier. Mutual funds provide more diversification than most investors could achieve on their own. The fund manager also should be familiar with international investing and have the resources to research foreign companies. The fund will handle currency conversions and pay any foreign taxes, and is likely to understand the different operations of foreign markets. Like other international investments, mutual funds that invest internationally often have higher costs than funds that invest only in U.S. stocks.

Study Your Options

Now that you have a greater understanding of the different types of investments you should be considering when thinking about profiting from China's economic boom, take the time to choose the one that will work best for you. It's important to study your options and make an informed decision before you invest your money. Read on to continue your guru training and take a deeper look at how to identify opportunity in Chinese stocks and maximize the potential of your investment choices.

CHAPTER

18

Identifying Opportunities in Chinese Stocks

There are three methods of gaining wisdom. The first is reflection, which is the highest. The second is imitation, which is the easiest. The third is experience, which is the bitterest.

—Confucius

We learn in this chapter a system that you can use to analyze individual Chinese stocks and we examine the challenges experienced by investors as they do so. In Chapter 19, we will discuss how to combine these stocks into a working portfolio and manage its risk, that is, you will learn how to build a China Stock Guru portfolio. We will also review opportunities among China-based mutual funds and exchange-traded funds (ETFs). But first, we need to know how to look at a Chinese stock and identify whether we have found treasure or trash.

Regardless of whether you ultimately decide to build your own China portfolio with individual stocks, or choose instead to access a ready-made portfolio of China stocks by investing in a mutual fund or ETF, the process that I discuss in this chapter can make you a savvier investor and help you profit from China's economic boom.

Measuring Your Stock's Value

I remember quite well, and I suspect you do, too, back during the heyday of the United States' dotcom craze, when young investment analysts, often fresh out of college, would appear on financial television networks and glorify the newest breed of Internet-related companies. Although the companies hyped were often different, the underlying story was generally the same. The typical pitch went something like this: "The Internet is the biggest technology innovation of our time and will undoubtedly revolutionize our business and personal lives. Because the Internet industry is so new, we needn't worry about traditional measures of investment value such as book value, price to earnings multiples, and profitability."

I believe these traditional measures are crucially important. It is worth your time to understand them because these measures will make the difference between a stock market bust like the dotcom craze and the potential to profit from growing corporate giants in China.

Traditional Definitions of Stock Value

- *Book Value*   A company's book value is calculated by using this formula: Assets – Liabilities = Book Value.
- *Book Value per Share*   A company's book value per share is calculated by using this formula: Book Value/Shares Outstanding.
- *Price to Book Ratio*   This figure is determined by using this formula: Price per Share/Book Value per Share.
  - Generally speaking, the lower the Price to Book Ratio, the better the value the stock represents. Value investors like myself generally are looking to buy stocks at Price to Book Ratios that are below the average for the market at any given point in time.
- *Price to Earnings Ratio*   This figure is determined by using this formula: Price per Share/Earnings per Share.
  - Generally speaking, the lower the Price to Earnings Ratio, the better the value the stock represents. Value investors like myself generally are looking to buy stocks at Price to Earnings Ratios that are below the average for the market at any given point in time.
- *Price to Sales Ratio*   This figure is determined by using this formula: Price per Share/Revenue per Share.

♦ Generally speaking, the lower the Price to Sales Ratio, the better the value the stock represents. Again, value investors like myself are generally looking to buy stocks at Price to Sales Ratios that are below the average for the market at any given point in time.

For a time, the dotcom hot stock approach seemed to work. Countless numbers of investors became convinced of the power of this new technology. Billions were poured into the new industry and into the unproven stocks that represented it. Month after month, Internet stocks would rise in price, despite the fact that these companies were burning up their cash reserves faster than a bunch of drunken sailors on shore leave so they could finance the massive business losses and the hard-to-justify salaries of their management team. The lack of corporate profitability and the unrealistic stock valuations assigned to these speculative investments ultimately became their undoing, and the undoing of many of their investors' personal fortunes.

The moral of this story is this: Just because a significant new trend emerges that will change the world's economic landscape doesn't mean that we can succeed if we fail to identify the stocks that will benefit from that trend, or if we pay too much to buy those stocks. As investors, we will not succeed without doing our shareholders' homework. As you look at the stock values created by the economic rise of China, you must remember that some stocks will become gems and a great many stocks will ultimately become junk in the marketplace. Your investment success and ability to profit from China's economic boom depends on your skill at differentiating between the two.

The Three Keys

I suggest that you look at three measures to identify the value of a Chinese investment. The three measures I look at most closely are the Price to Earnings Ratio, the Price to Book Ratio, and the Price to Sales Ratio. Using all three of these traditional measures in combination allows me to identify the nuggets of gold as I pan through the sea of Chinese stocks. To illustrate this point, let's look at an example of this process.

In late February 2007, the Chinese markets fell hard, based on a prediction of a recession in the United States, announcements made by the Chinese government about changes in stock trading rules, and comments made by former U.S. Federal Reserve Chairman Alan Greenspan in a speech he gave in Hong Kong. My research team in China immediately informed me of these events. On the morning of this pullback, I received calls from CNN wanting my thoughts on what this all meant for investors before the stock markets opened in the United States. As a result, I quickly ran an analysis of all of China's top companies using the three measures of value I recommend, the Price to Earnings Ratio, the Price to Book Ratio, and the Price to Sales Ratio. Had you been a subscriber to my *China Stock Digest,* you could have saved yourself some math, as I immediately completed this exercise and informed my subscribers of the results of my analysis and provided a list of specific actions to consider. My answer to CNN was based on my review of the three measures of stock value of China's top industrial companies. Experience has proven that any viewer serious about investing in China had just been handed a gift.

For example, one of the companies I reviewed in March 2007 was the Aluminum Corporation of China (ACH), China's premier aluminum producer and one of the country's best run and most profitable industrial companies. Tables 18.1 and 18.2 show what my analysis revealed.*

Based on even a cursory review of market value, my analysis indicated we could buy shares in one of China's premier high-growth blue chip companies at a Price to Earnings level of less than half what we would pay for a U.S. company. Of course, the U.S. company might possibly have lackluster growth in a mature industry. Based on my

Table 18.1   Stock: Aluminum Corporation of China (NYSE: ACH)

Price on March 1, 2007	$23.00/Share
Price to Book Value	2.4
Price to Earnings	8.0
Price to Sales	1.2

---

*This example is for illustration purposes only, and is not intended to recommend the purchase of this or any other stock. The attractiveness of a stock for investment purposes is a dynamic process. The example that follows recognizes the process used to identify an investment opportunity for a stock at a particular historic point of time. The current price and attractiveness of this stock or any other may have no relation whatsoever to its past price or investment viability.

Table 18.2   Comparison to the Typical American Company in March 2007

Price to Book Value	2.7
Price to Earnings	17.8
Price to Sales	1.4

findings, I immediately sent out an alarm to my newsletter subscribers to buy this company. This method of stock analysis was quite effective, as the stock has since proceeded to more than double in value.

Stick with Traditional Values

I go through all this explanation to make a point: Even in China, the world's fastest-growing major economy, we need not abandon time-tested, successful approaches to identifying value in stocks as we build our portfolios. When making our move into China, we can ignore many of the analysts we see on financial television programs. Let them claim you can forget about traditional value measures in China. That's the same old story they gave about the Internet a decade ago, and that they gave about the biotech industry the decade before that. We know better, thank you very much.

When building our portfolio in China, any investor who ignores traditional measures of value does so at his own peril (see Figure 18.1).

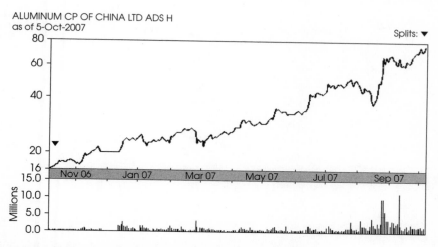

Figure 18.1   Identifying Stock Values Equals Profits
Source: Reproduced with permission of Yahoo! Inc. YAHOO! and the YAHOO! logo are trademarks of Yahoo! Inc. (http://finance.yahoo.com/).

CHAPTER 19

Assembling Your Portfolio and Managing Risk

If China continues to press ahead toward a free-market economy, it will surely propel the world to new levels of prosperity. Much of how the world will look in 2030 rests on this outcome.

—Alan Greenspan
The Age of Turbulence: Adventures in a New World

Now that you know how to identify the value in Chinese stocks, it is time to assemble your portfolio. In this chapter, I give advice on how to choose stocks for your portfolio and assign them the appropriate weight. I also provide advice on the parameters of the three methods an investor can use to access financial opportunities that we discussed in previous chapters. When building your portfolio, it is important to be mindful of the increased risk and volatility associated with the great financial rewards that you may receive.

Building a China Stock Guru Portfolio

In our last chapter, I illustrated the process I use to analyze and differentiate opportunities among China-based American Depositary Receipts. In addition to using this fairly straightforward process of financial calculation, I have the added advantage of having my own team of analysts inside China. This allows me access to another piece of the puzzle that is not always revealed by the numbers alone, namely, it keeps me current on consumer trends, government policies, and economic changes that may not yet be reflected in the numbers.

Having local knowledge is a distinct advantage in a society that is changing as quickly as China. It has allowed subscribers to my *China Stock Digest* newsletter to multiply their investments, often 200 percent or more on a single stock, which is far above the returns available in either the exchange-traded funds (ETFs) or from most Chinese mutual funds.

If building an individual stock portfolio and profiting from China's economic boom is your goal, you would be wise to receive firsthand knowledge of the occurrences unraveling in China as they happen. Before you do so, I recommend that you make sure that you have enough capital to own at least 10, but ideally 20, different Chinese stocks. (You can access some of my real-time research by visiting my web site, chinastockdigest.com, where you can get a free trial issue, to keep you on top of changes going on inside China.) This means you need to have investment capital of at least $50,000 or more. If you do not have sufficient investment funds to do this, I suggest that you focus on building your portfolio from mutual funds and ETFs.

When building a portfolio for one of my clients, whether they are a high net worth family or a corporate pension fund, I always make sure that I have purchased a wide variety of stocks so the portfolio will not get crushed should one of my recommendations fall short of expectations. As such, I recommend buying stock in at least 15 to 20 different companies, all with equal weighting in the portfolio. If you have the resources to make this type of investment, you can be quite successful. If buying 15 to 20 different names is out of your budget, let's examine our other choices, exchange-traded funds and mutual funds.

China's Top-Performing Exchange-Traded Funds

China-oriented exchange-traded funds are a quick and easy way to access the Chinese stock market. The two most popular funds for this purpose are the IShares FXI Index and the IShares EWH Hong Kong Index. As China becomes more prosperous, though, I am sure new funds will become available. Both of these index funds can be purchased through a regular U.S. brokerage account on any trading day. Let's look at bit closer at both of these funds.

- *FXI—The IShares FTSE Xinhua China 25 Index* This fund seeks investment results that generally correspond to the price and yield performance, before fees and expenses, of the FTSE/ Xinhua China 25 Index. The fund generally invests at least 90 percent of assets in the securities of the index or in ADRs or GDRs representing securities in the index. This fund can be located on any stock quote system using its trading symbol, FXI.
- *EWH—The IShares MSCI Hong Kong Index* This fund seeks to provide investment results that generally correspond to the price and yield performance of publicly traded securities in the Hong Kong market, as measured by the MSCI Hong Kong Index. (MSCI stands for Morgan Stanley Capital International, Inc., the creator of the index.) The fund normally invests at least 95 percent of assets in the securities of its underlying index and in ADRs based on the securities in its underlying index. It uses a representative sampling strategy to try to track the index. The index consists of stocks traded primarily on the Stock Exchange of Hong Kong Limited. It is nondiversified. This fund can be located on any stock quote system using its trading symbol, EWH.

The China-based ETFs have been among the top performers on Wall Street. Consider the performance of these funds in recent years in Table 19.1.

The advantage of both of the funds depicted in Table 19.1 is that you can access a basket of Chinese stocks quickly without having to think about, or research, the individual companies involved.

The disadvantage with both of these funds typically includes high price earnings ratios, which can significantly increase risk. Another disadvantage of ETFs is the associated problem of the weighting

Table 19.1   Top-Performing ETFs in China

Fund Name	Symbol	Thru 12/16/07	2006 Performance
IShares TR FTSE Index	FXI	53.8%	83.1%
IShares MSCI Hong Kong	EWH	35.6%	29.3%

Sources: Barclays Global Investors and MSN Money.

method that is used to structure these funds. Weighting by market capitalization, which is what we typically find in index funds, means a disproportionate concentration of money (and therefore risk) is placed in the companies having the largest total market value (also known as market capitalization). Risk is not spread evenly among all of the companies in the index, but is instead shifted to only some of the more concentrated companies.

Chinese ETFs are also often unmanaged. For example, the two funds depicted in Table 19.1 are not actively managed. That means no one is checking to see whether the companies included have released poor earnings or are undergoing challenges in their business units. If you want to receive active management on your China investments you must either build your own portfolio using ADRs or invest in China by using China-focused mutual funds.

Top-Performing Mutual Funds in China

A mutual fund is a company that pools money from many investors and invests the money in stocks or other securities or assets. The combined holdings the mutual fund owns are known as its portfolio. Each share represents an investor's proportionate ownership of the fund's holdings and the income those holdings generate.

A recent search of China-oriented mutual funds indicated dozens of these instruments with new ones coming out all the time. The advantage of investing in China stocks, by way of a China-based mutual fund, is that you save the time and effort of doing your own research. You also can pick up diversification and possibly avoid the overweighting problems found in the ETFs that attempt to mimic the China market indexes.

Many China-based mutual funds have been among the top performers on Wall Street. Consider the performance of the following funds in Table 19.2.

Remember, however, that mutual funds, just like any other investment, are not free from risk. When evaluating a mutual fund, it is important to investigate the fund's operating expenses, sales charges, and track record. One resource many investors find helpful when evaluating mutual funds is the research available from Morningstar, which is based in Chicago. You can access them through their web site at morningstar.com. One final point, when doing your research on China mutual funds, don't forget to apply the same type of price

Table 19.2   Top Performing Mutual Funds in China

Fund Name	Symbol	Thru 12/14/2007	2006 Performance
AIM China Fund Class A	AACFX	65.2%	42.79%
Mathews China Fund	MCHFX	60.8%	64.8%
Eaton Vance Greater China	EVCGX	56.8%	47.6%
Templeton China World	TCWAX	33.7%	40.9%
ING Greater China Class A	IFCAX	36.4%	48.8%
Fidelity China Region	FHKCX	22.9%	29.7%

Source: MSN Money/Google Finance.

earnings and financial ratio analyses that we discussed in the previous chapter on the fund's top holdings.

Risk Management Techniques

Emerging equity markets, like China, present special challenges for investors. The typical techniques many investors use to limit risk include quality (stock valuation metrics), diversification, and stop loss orders.

The starting point for limiting risk is building quality into your portfolio. In other words, you should not overpay for your holdings based on traditional stock valuation metrics such as the Price to Earnings Ratio, the Price to Book Ratio, and the Price to Sales Ratio.

Diversification is another effective tool, perhaps even the most effective tool, at our disposal in managing risk in our portfolio of China stocks. Investors often lack an awareness of the power of diversification. The typical investor understands that diversification may reduce volatility, but suspects that diversification simultaneously impairs returns. Diversification often functions to improve returns, not diminish them. Investors need to be educated about this potential dual benefit.

Diversification is not merely a matter of owning a couple of dozen different stocks. If all of these stocks have similar risk factors, such as being in the same asset class or industry, they will tend to move together. Therefore, when one stock is doing poorly, they will all tend to do poorly. Ineffective diversification is illustrated in Figure 19.1.

As long as the assets in a portfolio do not move together, you can achieve effective diversification. This point was proven by

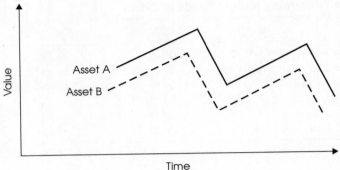

Figure 19.1   Ineffective Diversification

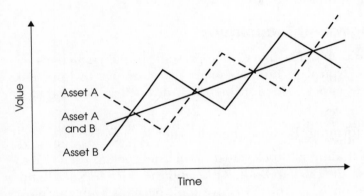

Figure 19.2   Effective Diversification

Harry Markowitz's Nobel Prize–winning theory, which shows that when the securities in a portfolio do not move together, the risks inherent in each security are reduced. Please note, however, that diversification does not assure a profit, or protect against loss in a declining market. Figure 19.2 shows how effective diversification would appear.

For the purpose of profiting from China's economic boom, the key to diversification is not to allow any one stock or industry to become a disproportionately high percentage of the portfolio. For example, if every stock in your China portfolio was in the Chinese banking sector, and China developed a banking crisis, your portfolio would suffer losses on a disproportionate basis. The goal with diversification is to select industries that would offset one another's performance. Likewise, if your Chinese stock portfolio was made up of only three or four companies, a crisis in any one company could destroy the profitability of the entire portfolio.

The final risk management tool we will consider is the stop loss order. A stop loss order is an order to sell a stock once the price of that stock drops below a specified level. When the specified stop price is reached, the stop order is entered to sell the stock at the next available market price.

The purpose behind stop loss orders is to create limits that will trigger a restructuring of your portfolio in a down market. When limits are reached, equities will be pulled out of your portfolio and moved to cash equivalents. Limits could be set to trigger restructuring whenever equities decline to a fixed percentage (for example, 10 percent of their prior valuation).

Essentially, the creation of limits is a stop-loss mentality, which means that you do not let your losses spiral downward while you pray for a magic recovery to save you. Failure to set restructuring limits has destroyed more retirement portfolios than any other factor I have seen during my years as a financial adviser.

With a stop loss order, you do not have to actively monitor how a stock is performing. Because the sell order is triggered automatically when the stop loss price is reached, however, a sale could be triggered by a short-term fluctuation in a stock's price. Also it is important to know that in a fast-moving market, the price at which the trade is executed may be much different from the stop price.

Remember, setting restructuring limits is easier said than done with mutual funds because there is no way to place stop loss orders on the typical open-ended mutual fund. Therefore, either you or your adviser must constantly monitor your portfolio's performance to avoid potentially devastating losses.

The use of stop loss orders will theoretically reduce the level of risk in your portfolio. There are limitations to stop loss orders, however, which at times make them ineffective. The first problem is that setting a stop loss order does not guarantee that you will sell your stock at the preset stop price. When a stop order triggers a sale, your stock will trade at the next *available* price, which may be far below the price you set. Second, in a highly volatile stock (as is often the case in China's emerging market) you may find yourself selling a good stock that fluctuates within a normal price range, only to learn later that it has appreciated after your stop sale and you are unable to repurchase it at anywhere near the discounted price you sold at. Therefore stop losses should be used only with caution and a great deal of forethought.

The Bottom Line

Using the tools of risk management covered in this chapter cannot guarantee you will never have a loss in your portfolio, but when they are used proactively, they will go a great way to lessening the likelihood and pain from a market decline.

Conclusion: A Peek at Your Guru Future

It is not the strongest of the species that survives, nor the most intelligent, but the one most responsive to change.

—Charles Darwin

Imagine, for a moment, that you have a time machine. Suppose it could take you into the future, say 50 years from now, to see what life in the United States would be like. Or, should you command it to do so, it could instead take you to ages past where you could seize an investment opportunity, unrecognized by the common people of that era.

To make things even more interesting, what if you were to use such a machine to visit the United States at the start of its Industrial Revolution? Knowing what you know today, you would likely buy stock in the companies destined to be the great U.S. industrial giants for mere pennies on the dollar, companies like General Electric, for example, which in 1896 became one of the first members in the newly formed Dow Jones Industrial Index.

Perhaps the Roaring Twenties are more your style. Perhaps you would choose instead to travel to the United States in 1925, where you could make a measly $500 investment in the Dow Jones Industrial Index. Had you used your time machine for that purpose, you would be a multimillionaire today. Think of the financial power you would have. But alas, dear reader, we have no machine to transport us to the past, and no such opportunities are in easy reach because the U.S. Industrial Revolution ended more than a century ago. Today's United States has a stable, mature economy, one that can help an investor maintain a certain standard of living. But today's United States is not going through the type of fundamental shift that created the fortunes of the nation's Gilded Age, and established family dynasties like the Rockefellers, the Morgans, and the Vanderbilts.

Do not despair over our lack of a time machine to take us to ages past. We have something almost as good. When we look closely at the tectonic shifts in world economic events brought about by the fall of the Bamboo Curtain in China, we at least will have a semblance of a time machine that will allow us to see a great deal of the future to come. Armed with that vision, we can make some shrewd financial decisions today that may have as much impact on our personal fortunes as if our time machine could take us back to 1896 to invest in General Electric when it was added to the Dow Jones Industrial Average or even to 1925 to buy into the Dow Jones Industrial Index.

The book you have just completed provides you with a view of the future. It is a future where the United States is no longer the world's largest economy. Like the British Empire of a hundred years ago, the United States must, like it or not, make room for the prosperity of other upcoming nations. The next century for the United States is likely to be a time in which gasoline and housing prices could easily double or triple from where they stand today. It is a period in which the formerly rich nations will pass the torch to the hungry new waves of capitalists. It is a time in which you will either have created the personal fortune required to thrive and protect your family, or you will join the uninformed masses that will be tossed about by the currents of world events.

It is undeniable that China will have the world's largest and most prosperous economy within a generation. Just as if we had a time machine to visit the dawn of the United States Gilded Age, we have the ability to seize the opportunities created from this fundamental shift in the world's economic environment and harness their success to help build our own fortunes.

I hope that I have provided you with the vision and the tools needed to profit from China's capitalist revolution. If you need a helping hand or a word of encouragement, please visit my web site, chinastockdigestguru.com, which has abundant resources to keep you on the right path. I even have a gift for you there to help you get started.

The future lies ahead and beckons you to become its master. Will you answer its call?

Notes

Chapter 1 Sunrise in the East

1. *World Wealth Report,* Merrill Lynch Capgemini.
2. *Hurun Report,* October 2006; Rupert Hoogewerf, *2007 China Rich List,* October 2007. Also, *China Daily,* October 10, 2007, and Forbes/Bloomberg, March 25, 2007.
3. "China's Richest Is a Woman," *Hurun Report,* October 6, 2007; *2007 China Rich List,* magazine commentary.
4. Jonathan Worrall and Peter O'Shea, *From Wall Street to the Great Wall* (Hoboken, NJ: John Wiley & Sons, 2006), 41.
5. National Development and Reform Commission, May 7, 2007.
6. National Bureau of Statistics, July 11, 2007.
7. Oded Shenkar, *The Chinese Century* (Upper Saddle River, NJ: Wharton School Publishing, 2004), 2.
8. Clyde Prestowitz, *Three Billion New Capitalists* (New York: Basic Books, 2005), 74.
9. allcountries.org/china_statistics.
10. *BBC News,* September 19, 2001.
11. Thomas L. Friedman, *The World Is Flat* (New York: Farrar, Straus and Giroux, 2005).
12. Carl E. Walter and Fraser J.T. Howie, *Privatizing China,* Second Edition (Hoboken, NJ: John Wiley & Sons, 2006), 3.
13. *Hurun Report,* October 2006.
14. *CIA World Factbook,* 2007.
15. *VOA News,* July 16, 2007.
16. National Development and Reform Commission, July 11, 2007.
17. Beijing Municipal Bureau of Statistics.
18. *The Economist,* April 13, 2007.
19. National Development and Reform Commission, October 11, 2006.
20. The UN poverty benchmark is an income of less than $1 a day.
21. pbs.org, January 11, 2006.
22. greyglobalgroup.com.
23. National Development and Reform Commission, July 11, 2007.
24. *People's Daily,* September 20, 2006.
25. World Bank, 2006 report as quoted by CIA World Factbook 2007.
26. *CIA World Factbook,* 2007.

27. *CIA World Factbook*, 2007.
28. FAO, fao.org/docrep/009/ag088e/AG088E04.htm.
29. *People's Daily*, April 5, 2006.
30. Keating's keynote address to the World Banker Summit, Jakarta, Indonesia, March 26, 2007.
31. *Thomson NewsEdge*, August 30, 2006.
32. National Development and Reform Commission, Ma Kai statement, May 7, 2007.
33. From Paul Craig Roberts, chairman of the Institute for Political Economy and Senior Research Fellow, Hoover Institution, Stanford University. Roberts relied heavily in his remarks on statistics from Morgan Stanley. Roberts was assistant secretary of the treasury for economic policy from 1981 to 1982. Quoted from newsmax.com.
34. *The Economist*, April 1, 2007.
35. *Industry Week*, July 11, 2007.
36. Testimony by C. Fred Bergsten before the Hearing on U.S.-China Economic Relations Revisited, Committee on Finance, United States Senate, March 29, 2006.
37. Carsten Holz, *Far Eastern Economic Review*, April 2006.

Chapter 2 Sunset in the West

1. From comments by Chinese Minister of Commerce, Bo Xilai, July 13, 2007.
2. From comments by Chinese Minister of Commerce, Bo Xilai, July 13, 2007.
3. Paul Saxena, dailyreckoning.com.au, May 9, 2007.
4. *The Telegraph*, United Kingdom, July 10, 2007.
5. dailyfx.com, Wednesday August 8, 2007, was also quoted in Marketwatch.com, August 8, 2007.
6. BBC, http://news.bbc.co.uk/1/hi/world/asia-pacific/1330223.stm; japan-guide .com/e/e2321.html.
7. *China Economic Review*, August 9, 2007.
8. *Shanghai Daily*, August 12, 2007.
9. U.S. Commerce Department.
10. U.S. Commerce Department.
11. McKinsey Global Institute, *The U.S. Imbalancing Act: Can the Current Account Deficit Continue*, June 2007.
12. *USA Today*, "Taxpayers on the Hook for $59 Trillion," May 29, 2007.
13. Paul Craig Roberts, *Moving Our Economy Offshore*, vdare.com/roberts/economy_ offshore.htm, February 18, 2004.
14. U.S. Department of Labor, *The Ten Fastest Growing Occupations—2004–2014*.
15. Dr. Malcolm Cook, *The Future of the Australia-China Relationship*, Lowy Institute of Australia, July 2007.
16. Dr. Geoff Raby, *The Chinese Economy: Impact on Korea and Australia*, Lowy Institute of Australia, August 4, 2005.
17. Liao Xiaoqi, Vice Minister of Commerce, July 15, 2007.
18. Stanford University's economist Ronald McKinnon, in the *Journal of Turkish Weekly*, August 15, 2007.

19. *China Daily* report on Chinese Vice Minister of Commerce Liao Xiaoqi, July 15, 2007.
20. Voice of America report by David Gollust, U.S. Department of State, July 24, 2007.
21. *Associated Press–International Herald Tribune* quotes from Greg Sheridan, foreign editor of *The Australian,* September 7, 2007.
22. businessroundtable.org, We Can't Stand Still: The Race for International Competitiveness, March 8, 2007.
23. Ibid.
24. Pew Global Attitudes Project, *Global Opinion Trends: 2002–2007,* July 24, 2007.
25. Chinese government's official web portal, gov.cn.
26. *U.S. News and World Report,* "China is Making Friends and Influencing People," July 29, 2007.
27. *Military Power of the People's Republic of China,* Defense Department annual report, May 2007.
28. All figures are from *Military Power of the People's Republic of China,* Defense Department annual report, May 2007.
29. *The Star,* Malaysia, August 8, 2007.
30. *Military Power of the People's Republic of China,* Defense Department annual report, May 2007.
31. Ibid.
32. Executive Director Gal Luft, The Institute for the Analysis of Global Security, *Los Angeles Times,* February 2, 2004.
33. Ibid.
34. *Agence France Press,* "China, Russia, Central Asian Leaders Tout New Strength," 2007.
35. Chinese Academy of Social Sciences, *People's Daily,* August 16, 2007.
36. Research and development investment rose to 1.4 percent of GDP in 2006, according to the Intellectual Property Research Centre at Shanghai Jaiotong University.
37. David KirkPatrick, *Fortune,* July 9, 2007.
38. IBM news release, October 12, 2006.

Chapter 3 Breaking the Chains of the Bicycle Kingdom

1. Theautochannel.com, August 17, 2007.
2. Shaun Rein, *Fashionably Sensitive Chinese Investing,* China Market Research Group, March 5, 2007.
3. *International Herald Tribune,* "Luxury Brands Upbeat on Chinese Market," May 22, 2005.
4. The Federation of the Swiss Watch Industry, February 5, 2007.
5. Professor Jonathan Unger, Contemporary China Centre, Australian National University, *Far Eastern Economic Review,* April 2006, 27–31.
6. Ken Lam, McKinsey Consulting, *China Economic Review,* August 29, 2007.

7. National Bureau of Statistics, China Knowledge Online, chinaknowledge.com/news/news-detail.aspx?cat=general&id=11209, October 30, 2007.
8. Credit Suisse Bank, *Times of Oman*, March 24, 2007.
9. Arthur Kroeber, Dragonomics Research, *China Economic Quarterly*, May 9, 2007.
10. Jonathan Anderson, chief economist for UBS, *BusinessWeek*, May 9, 2007.
11. Shai Oster, "Property Owners Feel Right at Home in China," *Wall Street Journal*, March 14, 2007.
12. *Xinhua*, "Property Management Regulation Amended," September 2, 2007.
13. David Dollar, World Bank China Director, *The Economist*, April 1, 2007.
14. *China Daily*, "China Faces Labour Shortage in 2010," May 12, 2007.
15. Don Lee, "Manufacturers Taking Flight," *Los Angeles Times*, August 18, 2006.
16. Lou Dobbs of CNN and his staff have apparently made it an editorial practice to use the term *Communist China* as often as possible, disregarding the term's irrelevance.
17. Global Policy Forum, "China Says Absolute Poverty Is Eliminated, but Millions Are Grindingly Poor," November 17, 2000.
18. *People's Daily*, "China Wealth Gap Yawning." This article quotes *Xinhua* as an official source for its observations about the Chinese wealth gap. August 7, 2007.
19. James Kynge, *China Shakes the World*. (Boston: Houghton Mifflin, 2006).
20. *BusinessWeek*, "China Bank Bailout," January 26, 2004.
21. *Xinhua-Forbes*, "Bumper Year for State-Owned Enterprises," February 21, 2007.
22. *China Daily*, "SOE Heads' Careers Linked to Green Targets, August 30, 2007.
23. *China Daily*, "China Fights Against SOE Monopolies," June 25, 2007.
24. *Business Times*, "China's State Share Reform to Pass Tough Test," March 24, 2007.
25. *Wall Street Journal*, "China Seeks Advice on Health Overhauls," May 1, 2007.
26. *Fortune*, "China Goes from Red to Gray," June 20, 2006.
27. Professor Jonathan Unger, Contemporary China Centre, Australian National University, *Far Eastern Economic Review*, April 2006.

Chapter 4 The Coming Financial Flood

1. Global Manufacturer Trade Directory of China manufacturers, China suppliers, and China exporters.
2. businessroundtable.org.
3. C. Fred Bergsten, Bates Gill, Nicholas R. Lardy, and Derek Mitchell, *China The Balance Sheet: What the World Needs to Know Now about the Emerging Superpower* (New York: Public Affairs Books, Center for Strategic and International Studies and the Institute for International Economics, 2006).
4. *Washington Times* review of *The China Dream: The Quest for the Last Great Untapped Market on Earth*, by Joe Studwell (New York: Grove/Atlantic, 2002), April 14, 2002.
5. *People's Daily*, "China Is Alibi of World Textile Trade Friction," September 17, 2005.

6. Jim Mann, *Beijing Jeep: A Case Study of Western Business in China* (New York: Simon and Schuster, 1989).

7. *Washington Times* review of *The China Dream: The Quest for the Last Great Untapped Market on Earth*, by Joe Studwell (New York: Grove/Atlantic, 2002), April 14, 2002.

8. *Centre d'Etudes Prospectives et d'Information Internationales*, Paris 2007.

9. James Kynge, *China Shakes the World* (Boston: Houghton Mifflin, 2006). Kynge eloquently describes the disassembly of factories and mills in Germany and the United States, following them to China where they are rebuilt, and explaining the aftereffects on Western economies.

10. *USA Today*, "Force of China's Impact Grows in USA," December 12, 2006.

11. World Health Organization, "Chinese Air Pollution Deadliest in World, Report Says," *National Geographic News*, July 9, 2007.

12. C. Fred Bergsten, Bates Gill, Nicholas R. Lardy, and Derek Mitchell, *China The Balance Sheet: What the World Needs to Know Now about the Emerging Superpower* (New York: Public Affairs Books, Center for Strategic and International Studies and the Institute for International Economics, 2006).

13. *China Daily*, Qiu Baoxing, deputy minister of construction, June 7, 2005.

14. Zhao Baojiang, China Association of City Planning, August 30, 2007.

15. *China Daily*, "Green GDP Shown Red Signal," March 23, 2007.

16. *Xinhua*, "China to Reduce Pollution Discharge by 10 Percent," June 4, 2007.

17. *New York Times*, "GE Unit Gets China Contracts," March 8, 2003.

18. *China Daily*, "Wen Outlines Economic Strategies," September 7, 2007.

19. Duke University study of 2004 graduation rates from *Investors Business Daily*, December 12, 2005.

20. *People's Daily*, "Over $70 bln Foreign Investments Put into Hi-Tech," January 27, 2006.

21. Chinanews.cn, February 9, 2006.

22. Chinaview.com, September 28, 2006.

23. *BusinessWeek*, May 28, 2007; *Wall Street Journal*, National Congress of the Communist Party of China August 21, 2007.

24. *The Associated Press/International Herald Tribune*, "Intel Breaks Ground in China for US $2.5 billion Silicon Fabrication Plant," September 8, 2007.

25. *Xinhua*, "China Becomes Largest Supplier of Parts for Boeing," September 7, 2007.

26. Donald Greenlees and Nicola Clark, "China's ARJ21 Regional Jet Eyes Global Market," *International Herald Tribune*, people.com.cn, aerospace-technology.com.

27. Patent data from WIPO, SIPO, *China News*, *People's Daily*, and *Xinhua*.

28. Dan Koeppel, "Piracy on Parade at China Car Show," *The Age*, Australia, June 2007; *Popular Science*, "China's iClone."

29. *China National News*, "Chinese Company Accused of Copying BMW Car," September 7, 2007.

30. Oded Shenkar, *The Chinese Century* (Upper Saddle River, NJ: Wharton School Publishing, 2004).

31. *Wall Street Journal*, "Sorting out U.S.-China Relations," May 26, 2007.

Chapter 6 China's Booming Base—Manufacturing

1. C. Fred Bergsten, Bates Gill, Nicholas R. Lardy, and Derek Mitchell, *China The Balance Sheet: What the World Needs to Know Now about the Emerging Superpower* (New York: Public Affairs Books, Center for Strategic and International Studies and the Institute for International Economics, 2006).
2. Joseph Quinlan, managing director and chief market strategist of Banc of America Capital Management, *The Globalist.*
3. Yiannis G. Moustrous, Elliott H. Gue, and Ivan D. Martchev, *The Silk Road to Riches: How You Can Profit by Investing in Asia's Newfound Prosperity* (Upper Saddle River, NJ: Financial Times/Prentice-Hall, 2006).
4. Gordon H. Hanson and Raymond Robertson, *China and the Manufacturing Exports of Other Developing Countries,* Macalester College, July 2007.
5. Marco Bellandi and Marco R. Di Tommaso, *The Case of Specialized Towns in Guangdong, China,* in *European Planning Studies,* vol. 13, no. 5 (London: Routledge, July 2005), 707–729.
6. Clyde Prestowitz, *Three Billion New Capitalists* (New York: Basic Books, 2005).
7. James Kynge, *China Shakes the World* (Boston: Houghton Mifflin, 2006).
8. Oded Shenkar, *The Chinese Century* (Upper Saddle River, NJ: Wharton School Publishing, 2004).
9. *CNN Money,* "China Now Number 1 Source of Imports," September 11, 2007.
10. Thechinanews.net, "Double-Digit Growth for Chinese Textiles," March 25, 2007.
11. *Xinhua,* "Computer, Home Appliances Sectors See Over 5-fold Growth in Profits," September 12, 2007.
12. Chinaview.cn, "China May Achieve Industrial Economy by 2015," January 28, 2007.
13. IBM Institute for Business Value, "Going Global: Prospects and Challenges for Chinese Companies on the World Stage," April 4, 2006.

Chapter 7 China's Auto Industry—In Full Gear

1. *Xinhua,* "China Auto Industry—WTO," August 10, 2007.
2. *San Francisco Chronicle,* "China's New Middle Class in Love with Cars—Big Cars," August 18, 2007.
3. Kelly Sims Gallagher, *China Shifts Gears: Automakers, Oil, Pollution, and Development* (Cambridge, Mass.: MIT Press, 2006).
4. *Shanghai Daily/China News Services,* May 24, 2006.
5. Kelly Sims Gallagher, *China Shifts Gears: Automakers, Oil, Pollution, and Development* (Cambridge, Mass.: MIT Press, 2006).
6. *China Daily,* China Association of Automobile Manufacturers, August 14, 2007.
7. *People's Daily.*

Chapter 8 China's Energy Industry—Red Hot

1. *The Economist/Thomson Dialog NewsEdge,* "China Economy Critical issues – Energy," July 27, 2007.

2. *Wall Street Journal,* "Sorting out U.S.-China Relations," May 26, 2007.
3. Marketwatch.com, "China's Crude Oil Imports Rise," May 7, 2007.
4. David Winning, "China's First Quarter Crude Imports Rise, More Growth Seen as Strategic Reserve Built," Marketwatch.com, April 10, 2007.
5. Poten & Partners, "Bloomberg: Sinopec May Hire More Supertankers than Exxon Mobil," *China Economic Review,* April 27, 2007.
6. The Bureau's report and a supporting report from the Customs General Administration of China was released in the West on May 16, 2007 in a Bloomberg story entitled "China's Oil Output Rises 2% as Demand Increases (Update 1)."

Chapter 9 China's Bonanza—Banking and Finance

1. *China Daily/Xinhua,* "Chinese Banks Report Profits of US $35.8b in 1st Half," stats from CBRC, October 6, 2007.
2. Fei Ya, "Public Banks a Remarkable Feat: Study," *China Daily,* June 22, 2007.
3. *China Daily,* "CBRC Outlines Current State of Banks," July 6, 2007.
4. *China Daily,* "Innovative Securities Dealers First-half Profits up 425 Percent," August 15, 2007.
5. Boston Consulting Group, April 25, 2007.
6. *China Economic Review,* "ICBC Becomes World's Largest Bank," July 24, 2007.
7. Alan Wheatley, "China's Buoyant Economy not Unsinkable," *Reuters,* June 29, 2007.
8. *International Herald Tribune,* "China to Let Nine Foreign Banks Incorporate," December 24, 2006.
9. Jonathan Stempel, "Bank of America, China Construction in Venture," *Reuters,* September 6, 2007.
10. *China Daily,* "Banks Face Foreign Peers," January 26, 2007, July 4, 2007.
11. *Xinhua,* "Overseas Banks in China Report Sharp Growth," August 18, 2007.
12. China Insurance Regulatory Commission, July 25, 2007.
13. *Singapore Business Times,* "China Could Be Key in Private Banking: Stanchart," June 26, 2007.

Chapter 10 China's Communications Revolution— Almost Free Speech

1. *Xinhua,* "70 Percent of Cell Phones Are Foreign Brands," September 5, 2007.
2. Ministry of Information Industry, "China Produced 348 Million Handsets in January-August Period," *China Daily,* October 6, 2007.
3. Stuart Corner, "China Largest Broadband Market by 2007," *Ovum Research,* September 2, 2006.
4. Xi Guohua, vice minister of information industry, "China has 144 million Netizens by March," *Xinhua,* May 17, 2007.
5. Credit Suisse and Wallace Cheung, "Online Game Market," *Reuters,* June 28, 2007.
6. *Xinhua,* "Computer, Home Appliances Profits Grow Five-fold," September 12, 2007.

Chapter 12 Shenzhen—China's Test City

1. All data are from the Shenzhen Stock Exchange.

Chapter 13 Shanghai—China's Own Manhattan

1. Steve Schifferes, "Creating a Global City," BBC, Shanghai, May 7, 2007.
2. *CEO-CIO China Magazine*, "China Business Feature: China—A Tale of Two Financial Cities," June 8, 2007.
3. Carl E. Walter and Fraser J. T. Howie, *Privatizing China: Inside China's Stock Markets* (Hoboken, NJ: John Wiley & Sons, 2006).

Chapter 14 Taiwan—The Breakaway Prodigy

1. *China National News*, "China Doing Roaring Trade With Rival Taiwan," January 17, 2007.
2. *Xinhua*, January 17, 2007.
3. CIA World Factbook, 2007.

Index